Art and Architecture in Discus

D0940362

FRANK O. GEHRY
KURT W. FORSTER

Edited by Cristina Bechtler
in collaboration with Kunsthaus Bregenz

Cantz

"It sounds as if it's going to be three hours with our legs crossed in Frank Gehry chairs. You go if you want."

Contents

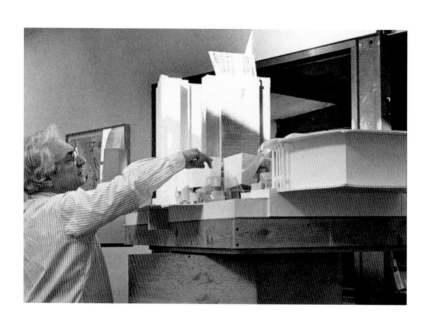

Foreword

Cristina Bechtler

"Sometimes you see a piece of paper changing shape as it travels in the wind, bending and flying, sliding and billowing with the forces playing upon it, like a ballet."[1]

The image of motion and lightness is a central element in Frank Gehry's architecture. In his office in Santa Monica, the tables are strewn with crumpled paper and building blocks, an invitation to sculptural "play." In addition to highly sophisticated computer technology, some of which he has developed himself, the "crafting" of sculptural forms still remains the point of departure for Gehry's creative process. His architecture not only transcends the dictates of the right angle, but points the way to the future with the recovery of humane building. Gehry succeeds like no other architect in responding to the anaesthetic-chaotic urban environment and integrating it into his designs, making it a self-evident part of the architectural dynamic. The museum in Bilbao, for example, connects the city with an unattractive industrial area on the river, while an originally ugly freeway bridge near the museum becomes a vital element in the overall urban conception. In contrast to the dogmas of modern architecture, based on structured reduction, a unified space grounded in central perspective and orthogonality, and symmetrical order, Gehry's high level of dialogic creativity enables entities and events to grow without predetermining the result.

Since the beginning of his architectural career, Gehry's remarkable ability to think sculpturally has led to associations with numerous artists and cultural figures; in the New York scene of the 1960s, relationships and friendships developed that continue to the present day. As a student in those days, he attempted to establish contacts between the departments of art and architecture, but to no avail—as Gehry himself remarked: "I always failed. The artists and the architects were in the same building, but never talked."[2] Still, relationships with artists developed outside the university and led to diverse collaborations with Richard Serra, Claes Oldenburg, and Frank Stella, who have lent unique expression to the synergy between art and architecture originally envisioned by Gehry.

The personal comments by Carl Andre, Walter De Maria, Sir Norman Foster, Jeremy Gilbert-Rolfe, Robert Rauschenberg, Richard Serra, Frank Stella, and Robert Wilson are published here for the first time.

Gehry's contacts to music and theater are diverse and intensive as well, involving costume and stage designs for a variety of musical productions. He is currently working on the "Disney Concert Hall" in Los Angeles, a project repeatedly pronounced dead—and now once again a project of superlatives. Virtually no other architect is so rooted in artistic introspection as he. Gehry is not only one of the most creative and ground-breaking architects of our time, but a fascinating personality as well.

Thanks are due above all to Frank Gehry—whose spontaneous hospitality is proverbial—for his immediate enthusiasm and enormous support for this publication project. Hearty thanks go to Kurt W. Forster, as well, for his extensive help and for conducting the dialogue in such a brilliant and effective way. We wish to thank the architects and artists who shared their impressions of Frank O. Gehry with us and for there perceptive and intriguing responses to our many queries. I am also grateful to Denise Bratton for editing the text, to Nanni Baltzer for checking facts, and to Keith Mendenhall for assembling the illustrations. Finally, very special thanks are due to Bernd Barde at Cantz Verlag and Edelbert Köb at the Kunsthaus Bregenz for their constant and enthusiastic support for this series.

1 Kurt W. Forster in the following dialogue, p. 89.
2 Frank O. Gehry in the following dialogue, p. 54.

The Architect Who Fell Among the Artists

Kurt W. Forster

The studio of Frank O. Gehry is located in a commercial district of Santa
Monica, California, near a hospital complex, across from the Department of
Motor Vehicles, and in the midst of media and entertainment industry offices.
In a neighborhood full of lumber yards and hardware stores, the office occu-
pies the second floor of a nondescript structure that Gehry personalized by
cladding it in sheet metal and fitting it with a catwalk that spans the facade.
A crowded parking lot stretches across the length of the building, and the
studio entrance, one among identical, run-of-the-mill doors, holds little of the
promise one might expect. When one reaches the top of the metal stairs,
the somewhat humdrum impression one has already gained is confirmed.

Frank O. Gehry, Studio, 1998, Santa
Monica, California

Frank O. Gehry, Studio, 1998, Santa
Monica, California

Frank O. Gehry, Studio, 1998,
Santa Monica, California

I imagine large tailoring shops looked like this in times past. No ostentatious
foyer, no fancy reception area, just the goods and the diligent workers who
produce them. To call the studio 'workaday' is to put no fine point on the
atmosphere of the shop, but it is precisely the no-frills ordinariness of the
place that invites one to get down to business without delay.

Unceremonious by nature, Frank is ever ready to jump into the fray of a discussion. When Cristina Bechtler and I visited him in the summer of 1997,
we had set out to raise some specific issues. And, though we were happy
to hear him speak on many more topics than we had come to discuss, he
never strayed very far from the subject that interested us the most: his
experiences with clients and his collaborations with artists. With colleagues
and patrons alike, he has developed a unique rapport, to be sure. But as
he spoke of his education and of the role art had played in the search for
his own persona, we realized how ultimately defining his acquaintances with
artists had been for his development as an architect. When Gehry was a
student, artists represented something approaching the incarnation of personal freedom in American culture. Money could buy you liberties, politics a
share of power, and Hollywood notoriety and fame, but all of these bland-
ishments exacted the same heavy toll: the sacrifice of personal freedom.
Only artists seemed able to win privileges without incurring the terrible loss-
es that other careers entailed.

Gehry was a late-bloomer approaching forty years of age when he burst
upon the scene in 1978 with his own house in Santa Monica. And a small

scene it was at first. Almost another decade would pass before a series of private residences and a few modest institutional buildings began to indicate the bare outlines of his architectural ideas. It may no longer matter that the Pritzker prize he garnered in 1989 was slow in coming, but it is worthy of note that this recognition did not require the almost ritual sacrifice of precisely those qualities that most intimately reside in and define an individual. I believe that the most fragile component of Gehry's personality, namely his desire to be an artist, delayed as well as secured the professional recognition he now enjoys.

If it is the architect's desire to invent a way to build, then his client's symmetrical wish is to have a building. In this ineluctable parity between client and architect resides the problem of making architecture. An intriguing thought on this subject was expressed by the architect and theorist Filarete in the middle of the fifteenth century. In his treatise on architecture, dedicated to the Duke of Milan, he cast long passages of his text in the form of a dialogue between patron and architect. What he has to say about their relationship is dramatized by the dialogical nature of his discourse, reflecting not only the will to control external circumstances, but also the power to motivate the internal bearings of his interlocutors. More than half a millenium later, Filarete's reflections on how buildings are brought into existence still make worthwhile reading. His thoughts revolve around one essential question: How are buildings conceived? "Since no one can conceive by himself without a woman," he argues, "the building cannot be conceived by one man alone. He who wishes to build needs an architect. He conceives

Canaletto (Giovanni Antonio Canale), Capriccio with Rialto Bridge after Palladio's Palazzo Chiericati, and the Basilica palladiana, 1740–1745, Galleria nazionale, Parma

the building with him and then the architect carries it. When the architect has given birth, he becomes the mother of the building." Throughout premodern times, with only a very few exceptions, buildings carried the names of their patrons rather than that of their architects. The architect's authority over his offspring yielded to that of the patron virtually at birth, when the father's name imposed a patrilineal order upon the building. Probably few would spontaneously associate the figure of the architect with feminine qualities or maternal instincts. Filarete does so, but not merely in order to belabor his simile. His reflections extend the analogy of human conception and birth into the psychology of the architect-patron relationship with all the insight of a seasoned practitioner. And, one might add, with the guile he developed in the course of his dealings with Renaissance princes.

Filarete goes on to claim that "building is nothing other than voluptuous pleasure." Arguing with rhetorical flourish, he scores genuine insight into the workings of desire when he explains that, "however much a man indulges in building, he always wants to do more of it." The architect, for his part, must attend in every way to his building, neglect no detail, and spare no effort. He ought to be, in Filarete's words, "thoroughly aware of all the advantages of every slightest thing and every necessity. And, even though the patron ... should wish to save on expenses, if the architect knows that the building will be damaged thereby, he should never give his consent." Filarete's tale makes the patron look like a swain or a fool, or both. No surprise then that Sebastian Brant chastizes the man who miscalculates the

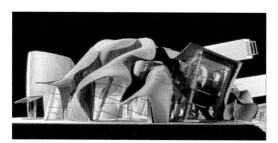

Frank O. Gehry/Philip Johnson, Lewis Residence, 1989–1995, Lyndhurst, Ohio

Giorgio Morandi, Still-Life, 1919, José Luis and Beatriz Plaza, Caracas, Venezuela

expense of his building in *The Ship of Fools* of 1494: while the workmen abandon their patron, he is tearing his hair out in despair over the useless fragment he built and the ruin he brought on himself.

When Filarete states unhesitatingly that "building is a voluptuous activity" that spurs one on to do more of the same rather than satiating one's desire, he acknowledges the nature of desire itself. It lies in the nature of desiring that it perpetually postpones its own fulfillment, or, as Filarete put it, "there is so much pleasure and desire in building that however much a man indulges himself, the more he wants." Goaded by the patron's wishes and stimulated by his own desire, the architect is brought face to face with his own boundless wishes and frustrations, as Gehry was during the years he worked on the Peter Lewis house (1989–1995). The project was finally abandoned in 1996, but not before Gehry rescued one of its chief component parts. He felt he had reached a 'breakthrough' when he invented a fluid foil to cover the atrium of the Lewis house. This windswept cape, originally modelled in waxed velvet, came to assume a unique shape. Gehry was satisfied because he had finally managed to create a singularly continuous foil. It was as if the sacrifice of the project as a whole had bestowed an unexpected reward on him: a single one of its elements assumed a shape more intimately his own than any he had ever produced.

Light as a feather yet dense as a cloud, almost Japanese in its collision with other parts of the Lewis house, but swirling nonetheless, this canopy became the very catalyst of desire. Karl Friedrich Schinkel had entertained a comparable notion, when he remarked in his notebook that instead of an architecture of tectonic firmity, there ought to be another one, able to convey different forces at play: "stretching, bending, compressing, extending, and so forth." Schinkel made his point by conjuring *intransitive* action, because he did not expect his desire to generate fixed properties in a building, but only to adumbrate its dynamic qualities. Similarly, the shape hovering over the atrium of the Lewis house possesses an almost infinite capacity for self-transformation. Its self-generating property springs from the very desire to invent. This invention reveals itself as a discovery, assuming an *analogous* character—analogous to the unselfconscious workings of nature. As a true *creation* of the architect, his invention affords him, and only him, that *"piacere voluptario"* about which Filarete wrote in the fifteenth century. With the singular shape of the swirling canopy over the atrium of the abandoned project, Gehry felt himself to be, perhaps for the first time, as unconditionally an artist in his own field as other artists are in theirs. Throughout his career, Gehry has never tired of presenting and discussing his work, but he has remained extremely reticent about "theorizing" at a time when theorizing one's work has often usurped the place of work itself. He prefers to muse about his experiences and string *impromptu* comments together into veritable *tales*. These tales are often spun from as many threads as bind the yarn of fables. It would be a pity if his stories were taken naively or literally, instead of being recognized as the *allegories* they are. They are allegorical in the original sense of "saying it another way," for only that other way can make the point of the story. In his tales Gehry aspires to an architecture just as filled with thought as his fish are *gefillt* with experience.

In some of the most affecting moments of the following conversation, Gehry touches on the vulnerable nature of his chosen identity as an *artist in architecture*. His artistic goals, that is, his commitment to collaborations with artists, remain phenomenal in a field that scarcely seems to tolerate such adventures. Never more stimulated or receptive than when in the company of artists, he accepts their criticism, and even tolerates their condescension and envy (to name just a couple of pertinent experiences). Whereas other architects feel deeply threatened by artists as soon as they overstep the 'boundaries' of their art and 'invade' the domain of architecture, Gehry has courted such encounters and even embraced their conflicts. Little concerned as he is with the alleged 'boundaries' of architecture, he does not insist that others respect the limits of their own media. Because the purpose of being an artist is to make something that could not be brought into existence without art, Gehry's desire to be himself found its (wish)fulfillment in being an artist.

At the same time as he sought the company of artists, he competed with them on turf of his own choosing. It wasn't really to be an artist among artists that he strove after, but rather to become an artist in the field of architecture. This may sound like a wish no one but Gehry himself could fulfill: as an architect, he could not escape the constraints of his profession, but as an artist he might be able to change the rules of the game. The rigors of his chosen trade are notoriously as hard on the purse as they are on the psyche. Gehry harks back to the difficulties in his schooling and the disappointments of his practice. As he tells the story, his many uncertainties led to a final *éclat* at Harvard. However, instead of merely stepping in line, he learned the hard way and earned his keep by doing a lot of humble work. This is surely the reason why he may appear to have been slow in maturing as an architect. Because he tends to think of architecture as an art, he is inclined to see art *within* (not added to or subsumed by) architecture. That is why he was able to carve out different spaces in the Guggenheim Museum at Bilbao where artists can create their own installations, and simultaneously make a building of uniquely "voluptuous pleasure."

The Quotations of Filarete are translated from the Italian after: Antonio Averlino detto Il Filarete, *Trattato di Architettura,* ed. by Anna Maria Finoli and Liliana Grassi, vol. 2, Milan 1972, p. 40ff. The quotation of Schinkel's Notebook is translated from the German after Goerd Peschken, *Karl Friedrich Schinkel. Das Architektonische Lehrbuch*, Berlin/Munich 1979, p. 32.

Conversation between Frank O. Gehry and

Kurt W. Forster with Cristina Bechtler

Santa Monica, California, August 24, 1997

FORSTER I suspect that your involvement with art and your collaboration with artists and other architects over a long period of time has had a great deal to do with the ideas you have developed. Out of this activity have come experiences quite different than those of a typical architect, and one could say that your work has developed over twenty years in a way that no other American architect's has. Again and again, your work intersects with that of other artists and architects, and these connections not only reach backward in time, but also extend outward to other cultures.

GEHRY Thinking of connections with other cultures, way back at the beginning, it was Gordon Drake who typified for me the American "GI" who went to Japan and got really excited about it, hadn't seen anything like it before, and came back enthusiastic. When I first arrived at USC, he had been teaching at the architecture school, and had just died in a skiing accident. For the students, he was kind of the "Jesus" of architecture, because he died at age thirty-five, so young. His death curtailed his lifework. But there were other faculty at the school who had been to Japan, who had also been bitten by the Japanese "beetle-bug," and who came back and waxed eloquent about the experience every time they got the chance to talk about it and show slides. When I started out, architects' lectures were always about Japan—especially the shrines. I thought places like Ryōanji and Ise were incredible. I was most impressed by the idea that they would rebuild Ise every twenty years. This was stunning. To me, it seemed relevant to what was happening then on the West Coast.

FORSTER Yes, there has been a long-standing connection to Japanese culture in California. Already at the turn of the century, the Greene brothers and later Frank Lloyd Wright were infatuated with Japan, and now, on the brink of the next millennium, the connection with the Pacific Rim is all the more tangible.

"If the architecture is as good as in Bilbao, fuck the arts!"
Philip Johnson

GEHRY But traditional Western classicism wasn't so exciting. I mean Los Angeles was a loosey-goosey place. It was growing fast, and there was an open-ended approach to that growth. You could say it was episodic, like the Chinese and Japanese scrolls and paintings David Hockney talked endlessly about in those days. This kind of thing was in the air, and it infected writers, filmmakers, artists, and musicians who moved here from somewhere else. They might have started to think this way before they came to Los Angeles, but when they got here, it moved, just like it did with Hockney.

FORSTER You used the term "open-ended." This is very interesting, because Los Angeles is open-ended in several ways, particularly in terms of expanded vistas. For Hockney, the scroll became the new visual frame, the exploded panoramic optic that replaced the standard western picture frame, which always implies the window.

GEHRY It's definitely the other side of that, and it makes sense here. I'm still fascinated with it. It still makes sense to me in these times, and it is suited to the idea of democracy, because it's an open-ended system that allows for freedom of interpretation and change. You can be a mystic, you know. If you look at Ryōanji, you can interpret it seven million ways. Every time you look at it, you can come up with a new interpretation—which you can't do with the Parthenon. Well, maybe you can, but it's not so easy to do.

FORSTER But it's interesting that you single out this open-endedness as the main door to understanding, because there are other aspects of Japanese art that have had great impact. For instance, slow and painstaking execution, or the cultivation of sustained efforts.

GEHRY These things are also interesting, but what I'm talking about is craftsmanship, the search, the truly relentless search for perfection. I loved that part of it, and it still fascinates me. I still try to achieve it, but you know, it doesn't work. It's linked to the belief that perfection is possible, and that you can improve with practice. If you make a stroke five million times, you can finally make it perfectly. But I think that the idea of open-ended structure in painting or music suggested an openness to interpretation and a freer way of dealing with the world. It suggested a way of dealing with the environment that to me was somehow easier for democracy to adopt than traditional Western classicism.

"I've always been interested in Frank's use of weightlessness, for example I think Gehry is beyond the modern but indebted to it in that in his work the weightless is not dependent on transparency. That goes to the question of the abstract nature of his forms and of his attitude to materials." Jeremy Gilbert-Rolfe

FORSTER Which didn't emerge under democracy.

GEHRY I know, I know. And that's why I have a problem with all the so-called "schools," the "isms," the "new simplicity," basically anything that pretends to prescribe a way of dealing with the world that is all-encompassing. They don't work for me; they don't make sense. The nicest thing about the last episode of postmodernism, even though I didn't like half of the stuff, was that.....

FORSTER Postmodernism suspended the notion that there was only one right way to do something, and that its logic was binding for everybody. Instead, it suggested infinite extension, perhaps even meaninglessness.

"The museum in Bilbao leads to a new era in building."
Sir Norman Foster

GEHRY I thought that a more open-ended system, one that suggested pluralism, was better. I love that. For example, I like Bob Stern, but not always what he does. I can be friends with a lot of people whose work I don't like, but who have a perfect right to do it. I don't like the idea of closing it down. The "new simplicity" suggests that we should close it down and get on with the work, because the work has nothing to do with social issues. It has nothing to do with the world we need to live in. But in this world, you cannot make things clean and simple and hermetic, you cannot simply "get rid of" crime. Architecture can't clean up the mess single-handedly, and what I see in the architecture that pretends to clean up the mess is contrivance. I don't think you can do it, that you can clean it all up so easily, sweep all the mess under the carpet. I think architecture should deal with the mess.

"I see Frank in this regard as an architect who has performed a certain kind of convergence between his discipline and the world at large." Jeremy Gilbert-Rolfe

FORSTER It's an absurd notion to expect people who have to operate under some of the most contingent circumstances of any profession to resolve what nobody else has been able to resolve.

GEHRY I say, "Go do your 'new simplicity' stuff. Try it! But be ready to take the rap if you can't deliver. If you're going to make a holier-than-thou promise, you'd better deliver. You probably can't, but try it anyway." I'm willing to go along with it and even support it, but I'm not going to do it. I just want the right to do something else.

FORSTER It's interesting to consider your connection to Japan and then to look at the reverse, let's say a Japanese architect like Tadao Ando, who is enamored of certain Western notions of composition even though he is celebrated for the particularly Japanese qualities he undoubtedly also manifests in his work. Still, he pursues that perfect object, which is curious when it suddenly appears in Central Europe as it does in Weil am Rhein. Maybe it doesn't really work, but it appears to be a perfectly European thing. It does not seem exotic.

GEHRY But I would make the point about Ando that he is, like all of us, subject to the client. The client is always part of what we do, and what Ando has enjoyed in Japan is a different kind of commission than we ever get in the United States, one that is involved with the landscape. His Himeji Children's Museum commands an entire park. It's as if I would be given a chance to do a pavilion or a building in the middle of Central Park. An architect never gets to do that in America. But Ando has had ten jobs like that.

Kobun-Tei House in the Kairaku-En Park,
Built in 1842 by Nariaki Tokugawa,
9th Lord of Mito, Japan

Kairaku-En Park, Mito, Japan

So it's a much different game, and it allows you to be infinitely more simple. If I was put in the middle of a park, I might defer to nature, too. I might say "nature is ten times more beautiful than anything I'm going to produce." I might even build something like Philip Johnson's Glass Pavilion. I might be moved to do something that I wouldn't do in the middle of Los Angeles, or even in the middle of Prague or Bilbao, because these are very different contexts. I would be curious to see what Ando would do in Prague or Bilbao.

FORSTER The American architects' context is more like the private garden than the park. You don't get to do grand, beautifully-situated buildings, but you've got this wonderful house on an estate and they decide to build a second house, creating a kind of still life. Your Winton guest house (1982–1987) in Wayzata, Minnesota, is such a project, isn't it? I can't help thinking of what you accomplished there under less than ideal circumstances.

GEHRY What I did there was to become very simple and respectful. But I had another problem there that you can't see. Again, it was the client. The clients were concerned about the fact that putting a new building on their land would make it look like they were subdividing their lot. Here they had this wonderful house on an estate and they decide to build a second house by another architect, because the original architect was not willing to do a second house for them.

FORSTER Yes. He wasn't willing to do it; he turned them down. Their first idea was to have Johnson do the guest house in the same style as the first

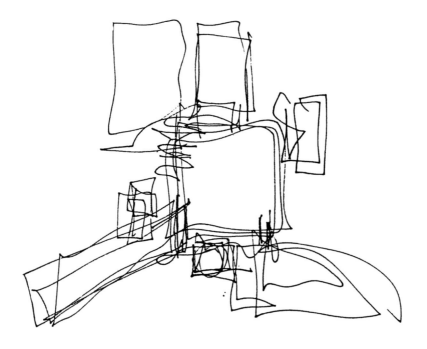

Frank O. Gehry, Winton Guest House, 1983

Frank O. Gehry, Winton Guest House, Interior, 1982–1987, Wayzata, Minnesota

Frank O. Gehry, Winton Guest House, 1982–1987, Wayzata, Minnesota

house, but he wouldn't do it. And they didn't want to have someone copy the Johnson house, because they're much more savvy than that, and it's not in their culture to have someone do a second-rate Johnson. So they decided to bring in someone else.

"Bilbao is one of the greatest achievements of architecture in the twentieth century. Conceptually it combines a collision of unknown spaces with an overlay of anthropomorphism. Imagewise it is as sinuous as a school of fish, covered with the curvature of a Boccioni bottle. It is an architecture of undefined invention and unlimited freedom." Richard Serra

BECHTLER Why did they bring you in?

GEHRY They read an article about my house in the New York Times. Their idea for the second house was that it could be a kind of potting shed to the main house, because a potting shed could be made out of cheap materials—corrugated metal, plywood—and thus wouldn't look like it was pre-empting the iconic superiority of the Johnson house. After all, it would just be a potting shed.

FORSTER Well, it's a classic scheme. Karl Friedrich Schinkel situated his Charlottenhof and its Gärtnerhaus at a certain distance from one another in Potsdam.

Karl Friedrich Schinkel, Charlottenhof,
1826, Berlin, Potsdam

Karl Friedrich Schinkel, Charlottenhof, Gardener's
House, 1829–1845, Berlin, Potsdam

GEHRY And then there was the Roman bath.

FORSTER Exactly. And, in fact, the two have enhanced one another, thanks precisely to their differences. You could say that the more difficult task was to design a subordinate building, and it may have had the effect of making the main building seem much more resolved, serene and independent.

GEHRY So my clients were hot on the trail of this funny potting shed, and they presented it to me as a potting shed project. If you look at my first models, they are like still lifes. I was into still lifes, but in this case, I made a log cabin, I made a funny green thing.

FORSTER Looks like an inverted pot, a flower pot.

GEHRY I forget, I did a whole bunch of stuff and it had chain-link and everything. It was a potting shed, and it was very rough and raw, and, well, very Rauschenberg in a sense.

Karl Friedrich Schinkel, Estate of Klein-
Glienicke, Casino, Berlin, 1824

FORSTER The rawness conjures up Rauschenberg's combines. That's a wonderful way of putting it.

GEHRY Yeah, it was like a Rauschenberg. I mean, after the fact it looked like or reminded me of a Rauschenberg.

"Frank Gehry's intuitive response to the economical, environmental and social needs is as remarkable as his sense of structure."
Robert Rauschenberg

FORSTER Perfect.

GEHRY But after I designed the potting shed, the clients really didn't like it. These are people who are very neat and clean, and they like finished stuff. They live in such a way that everything is cleaned up. They've got nice art, they've got a few Mies chairs. When they saw the potting shed, they couldn't relate to it. They just didn't like it. I couldn't tell what was going on, because they didn't really have words to express it. Finally, they said, "Well, it's not really right, it's not....." They dragged their feet, nobody would give approval, we couldn't get going. I was still trying to figure out what was going on, and finally, I went there and spent a weekend with them, stayed in the house with them, went out to dinner with them, watched how they lived, listened to their talk about the kids, listened to their dreams about what they were doing, and I realized that the potting shed didn't make any sense. What they really wanted, what had to happen so that the building wouldn't look like a subdivision of the land, was that it had to look like a sculpture. It had to look like a work of art. And that fascinated me even more.

FORSTER And that was right down your alley.

GEHRY Right down my alley: How could you play that game? Anyway, that's when I started thinking, well, if I made a still life, if I made a Morandi, with three bottles and two pots, three big bottles and three little bottles, in order for each piece to retain its objecthood, the thing had to have the crack, it had to have the separation, it couldn't be a continuous structure.

FORSTER And?

GEHRY One night, after this revelation had come to me, I called the client and said, "I know what to do now. I have an idea. But it's contrary to the weather and the climate, because in order to make this read like a sculpture, I have to have this crack. The parts of the building have to look like separate pieces that are barely touching. But that crack is going to be out in the snow and it's going to be a technical nightmare. But I think we've got to try it." And Mike Winton, the client, said, "Yeah, you're right, that's where we've got to go." He understood right away. He said, "Go for it, you're right, I understand." So then I did the building, the refinements. They loved it. The tenor of our meetings flipped into a productive mode. We met with several architects in the area to discuss the problem of the water getting into the crack and freezing and expanding. Everyone we talked to said we couldn't do it, that it was crazy to try. They said "Don't do it; it will be a disaster; it's not going to work." So I came home and built a full-size mock-up of the connection and discovered that it was absolutely conventional, it was as conventional a detail for a saddle and a roof as anything. When it was built at full scale, I realized I could actually build it, I could have a crack; it would read as a crack, with room to put your finger in. So that's how we did it. We built copper saddles that were seamless, put them in the crack. And it's never leaked. By coincidence, I had dinner with the Winton's last night, and they said again that the crack has never leaked.

"Bilbao is beautiful and inventive, which is more than enough, to satisfy me." Frank Stella

> **FORSTER** It's a great piece. In the same period, you were also doing Folly: The Prison Project (1983) at the Castelli Gallery in New York. It would make sense, because you had begun to explore similar possibilities with the Castelli folly and the Wosk residence (1981–1984) in Beverly Hills the same year.

"Clearly, there is no better architecture being built or conceived in today's world than Frank's." Frank Stella

> **GEHRY** Yes, I was lining up the elements.
> **FORSTER** You had them on your desk, you were putting them together, but you really hadn't yet composed a still life of them. And the wonderful thing with the still life, as opposed to just lining them up, is that the distances and the alignments among the parts become mobile, forming a sculptural composition.

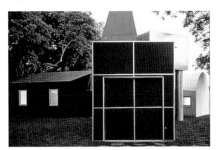

Frank O. Gehry, Winton Guest House, 1982–1987, Wayzata, Minnesota

Frank O. Gehry, Smith Residence, Model, 1981, Brentwood, California

GEHRY The prelude to all this was the Smith addition (1981) to the Steeves house in Brentwood (1959). I designed the house when I was just out of school, and then the Smiths wanted an addition done later on. That's where the idea for separate buildings first came up. The Smiths never built the addition; they got scared. But I used the idea when I did the Winton guest house a year later.

FORSTER But even there, the elements are really strung out; they haven't yet fallen into a subtle still life "composition."

GEHRY That model over there is the next phase of the idea. The brown one.

FORSTER Looks almost like the Schnabel house (1986–1989) in Brentwood.

GEHRY Well, not exactly. But it became the Schnabel house. It was actually a tract house (Tract house, unbuilt, 1982), you know.

FORSTER This is wonderful. Somehow, I never registered it before.

Frank O. Gehry, Steeves Residence, 1959, Brentwood, California

Frank O. Gehry, Schnabel Residence, 1986–1989, Brentwood, California

GEHRY It was for Barbara Jakobson. She was the curator for the Castelli follies, and after we did that, she said "let's do a tract house." The project for the house never materialized, but I designed it, I did it.

FORSTER The wonderful thing is that you can only recognize its latent form over a certain distance in time. The house for Ambassador Schnabel became just such a "hamlet" of rooms.

GEHRY But at that time, we couldn't do something like the Schnabel house.

BECHTLER How are the parts of the house connected?

FORSTER There aren't any connections.

BECHTLER No connections?

FORSTER No, you just go out of one room and into the next. This is California, remember. You don't have to worry about snow.

GEHRY But it's also Versailles! You see, because Versailles is just a string of rooms which were conceived to be "non-denominational." The king could do whatever he wanted with them. Because there was no such thing as plumbing and wiring. All he had to do was bring a bed and put it into the room, and voilà!

FORSTER That's it.

GEHRY But for me, the plumbing was a problem to solve. So I made the raised floor.

FORSTER So you could bring anything in from underneath.

GEHRY You come in from below, and that's why it was on a podium. And this could be the living room, or that could be the living room; this could be the bedroom, or that could be the bedroom. And then we did the classic courtyard, with these separate little pieces.

BECHTLER Where is the entrance?

GEHRY I don't know, probably here.

BECHTLER It could be, no?

FORSTER Well actually, in terms of how it works with the configuration of rooms as they are being used today, it was probably here.

GEHRY I think it was. I designed this for my own house. This was my fantasy for my own house. It was on an eighty-foot lot, which made me realize that I could do this on an eighty-foot lot, but not on a fifty-foot lot.

FORSTER Actually, coming back to the still life idea, your approach seems to have been conditioned by the fact that everything was divided up. In the end, you created a new creature altogether, one that no longer depends on the original parts.

GEHRY That's true.

FORSTER But think back to the early 1980s, when you began to deal with a series of components, each of them assuming a different role.

GEHRY But I wasn't the only one doing that.

FORSTER No?

GEHRY Jim Stirling was doing it, and Aldo Rossi was talking about Chardin's still life paintings.

FORSTER But with Rossi, the parts became miniatures. He placed a shed roof over a lot of little houses that were like toys in a kindergarten.

GEHRY We went different ways. I would be curious to know why that happens, that breaking down. I have a theory that it has to do with the search for a new urbanism, a new direction for the modern city, because the old forms don't fit anymore.

FORSTER This change came right on the heels of the mega-structures idea, which wiped out the notion of the city as a place where one wanted to be. So you, Rossi, and Stirling were all after the same thing?

GEHRY I think I related more to Stirling at the time, and probably also to Lou Kahn, who was interested in breaking down the building, except that when Kahn broke them down they kept their unity.

FORSTER Yes, he had the tendency to make them from similar parts.

GEHRY Yes, right.

**"Frank represents a break with all contemporary architecture.
His is not an architecture that arises from an older order. He is
the first to really break with the orthodoxy of the right angle."**
Richard Serra

FORSTER Therefore, the order of their composition became an abstraction, a mythical pursuit, something that was ultimately mathematical. Whereas Rossi, on the other hand, was after the idea of a still life and kept on miniaturizing it. He made dolls' houses out of them, little theaters. Remember his Teatrino?

GEHRY Yes, I do.

FORSTER Everything was gigantic and miniscule at the same time. The watchface became the hallmark of a surreal, scaleless setting.

GEHRY But you see, a breakthrough for me was to see him put the theater on the barge, so that it fell in with the context of Venice, with San Marco. It immediately made a still life of the entire city.

FORSTER The still life, again.

GEHRY But he also redefined Venice itself.

FORSTER By introducing a single element!

GEHRY Just one element. It was very powerful. I really got excited about that.

FORSTER In a sense, it was the fulfillment of Rossi's dream. First of all, the Teatro del Mondo was something that was floating away from an unknown former time and place. It was a tower with a theater inside.

GEHRY Made of wood, so it was cheap. I could relate to it because, at the time, I was doing things with cheap wood. And it had a very strong iconography. It held its own against all of Venice. It was like a lightning rod that took the energy of Venice to itself and became very powerful. And it suggested to me a new urbanism, too. It was the track we were all on, I think.

FORSTER Did you know that in his L'architettura della città of 1966, Rossi chose Venice as one of the key instances in support of his argument, especially a fictional Venice as Canaletto painted it, with bridges and buildings that didn't actually exist, but which he had painted into the townscape. Everything was real and recognizable as Venice, yet suddenly, in the midst of it, there appeared a bridge and the Basilica by Palladio.

GEHRY I looked at those paintings and at Chardin. Then I heard Rossi was looking at Chardin too. But I was also looking at Morandi.

FORSTER That one can tell.

Frank O. Gehry, Norton Simon Guest House,
1974–1976, Malibu, California

Frank O. Gehry, Norton Simon Guest House,
1974–1976, Malibu, California

Frank O. Gehry,
Norton Simon Guest House, Interior,
1974–1976, Malibu, California

Shiva as Lord of Dance (Nataraja), Tamil Nadu,
India, 10th Century, Norton Simon Museum,
Pasadena, California

GEHRY Morandi really excited me.

FORSTER Where did you come to see his work? There were very few Morandi exhibitions in America.

GEHRY Well, there was the big exhibition in San Francisco in 1981, and then I had the drawings book that came out around the same time.

FORSTER With your long-standing interest in still life painting and its architectural order, how did the notion of movement come into your work?

GEHRY That was my next move. It was a move to introduce movement, you might say. You wrote about it being related to dance, and I think you were right about that. My daughter studied dance, and I was interested in dance. But my interest in movement started about the time I was doing the Norton Simon guest house and gallery in Malibu, in 1976. He had that Indian figure of Shiva.

FORSTER The one with the many swirling arms?

GEHRY The one they claimed he stole from India and that he was supposed to give back after ten years. Norton Simon was a formidable human being. I was a struggling architect, and suddenly I was thrown into this billionaire's art scene. Simon was very powerful, all powerful, and scary, and I wanted very much to do a great job for him. I thought, "Man if I do this perfectly, I'm launched." Right. So it had that payoff laid on it, and it was scary. And I built it up even more. He and his wife, Jennifer Jones, and I used to sit around and talk about their guest house, about what they wanted. And then there was always the art game. He would bring in paintings and ask, "How much is this worth?" and "Which one do you like better?" It was fascinating to see how he approached art. He had a businessman's aesthetic, and we used to have fun with it. "Is this or that Cézanne the better one?" and "Is this or that Matisse better?" And he would have always two or three fabulous paintings on consignment. He always had the most beautiful paintings. But then one time he brought the Shiva home, and we sat looking at it, and I could have sworn I saw it move. I said, "The thing looks like it's moving." You'd look at it and turn around and you could swear it had changed position. And we started talking about that, and I realized that he just loved the idea of the illusion of movement. So, I thought, "OK, Norton, I'm going to show you. I can do that."

FORSTER I can "shiva" you?

GEHRY Yes. "If you like that, if that's what you like, I'm going to turn you on." So at one point, we had to put a trellis along the side of the guest house that fronted on the ocean. All I had to play with was wood, but I decided to make a trellis that looked like a pile of wood that had been laid on the roof, caught up in the wind blowing off the ocean, as if the wind had caught it and flung it into mid-air. The trellis would have captured this movement, and every time you looked at it, it would look different. That's what I was trying to do. I didn't know how to do it. I knew how to draw it, but I didn't know how to build it.

FORSTER Now, how would you have known how to draw it?

GEHRY I started drawing right away.

FORSTER But you make it sound as if it was the first time you had tried something like this. How could you suddenly draw it?

GEHRY I just started, I drew a lot. It was a way to get an impression.

FORSTER Of course, but that doesn't mean.....

GEHRY .....that I could make it look like it was moving?

FORSTER That's exactly what I'm wondering.

GEHRY The way I contrived to do it was to build it in situ. I would do a layer at a time. I did a drawing of the first layer of pieces of wood, and we built that. And then I went out and stared at it, and afterward I made a drawing of the next layer of pieces of wood, and we built that. And then I was starting the drawing for the third layer. No, I think I even got the third layer built, and Norton said, "Stop," because it was getting too expensive. He was a control freak. He wouldn't stand for it, it offended him that he was paying for this experiment and he didn't know where it was going to go, he didn't know if it was going to pay off. He said to me "There have been many great artists over time who have not been able to finish their masterpieces. I'm going to add you to the list." And so we stopped.

FORSTER But you had already built three layers of your "Mikado."

GEHRY Right, I had built enough layers to get excited. And there are pictures of it. Norton Simon's wife used to call it my "unfinished symphony," and I had to explain to her that she was just romanticizing the thing: Schubert's "Unfinished Symphony" was left unfinished because he died! I didn't die; Norton just pulled the plug! But anyway, once I was bitten by that idea, somehow I remembered seeing the Elgin Marbles at the British Museum in London. I was always fascinated by the warriors' shields, the way they press into the stone. When you look at them, you feel that pressure. Those two ideas led me on: the Shiva and the Elgin Marbles, and the experience of trying to do something like that with the little Norton Simon trellis.

FORSTER These two things are really very different. One is a kind of latent movement, where the shield is pressing into the stone, and the other one is movement trapped in its manifold stages.

Marcel Duchamp, Nude Descending a Staircase, 1912, Philadelphia Museum of Fine Art, Pennsylvania

GEHRY These are very different things.

FORSTER Yes, two very different things. These are probably the two oldest ways of imagining and representing movement. One conjures up what it takes for your arm to push against something, to offer resistance, an inner sense of the tension in your own body. The other recalls something too fleeting to be seen by the naked eye. You know that there were a number of experiments conducted in the late 1870s and 1880s, experiments with capturing movement with the camera, all those motion studies by Eadweard Muybridge.

GEHRY There was also Marcel Duchamp's "Nude Descending a Staircase."

FORSTER Daniel Libeskind drew such images, made up of a maze of objects you can only decipher because you realize that they are tumbling through one another.

FORSTER We haven't talked about anything without your mentioning the role of the client.

GEHRY I have realized lately, more than ever, that the process of making this stuff is the interesting thing. I just went to the opening of the EMR Communication & Technology Center building at Bad Oeynhausen (1991–1995). With that project, the client and the building group were extraordinary. The energy company was a great client. They said, "Energy is music, art, sculpture, literature." That immediately broadened the word energy for me. It wasn't just about the sun, the moon, and the stars; it was about a very beautiful experience with them. I went to the opening. I was very excited about the whole thing. Then, after that, I went to Bilbao, so I was immediately with the next client. And it was like a love affair, you know, "If you can't be with the one you love, love the one you're with."

Frank O. Gehry, EMR, 1991–1995,
Bad Oeynhausen, Germany

Frank O. Gehry, Iowa Laser Laboratory,
1987–1992, Iowa City, Iowa

Frank O. Gehry, Iowa Laser Laboratory,
1987–1992, Iowa City, Iowa

FORSTER A client in every port?

GEHRY Right. But over the years, there have been three buildings that I never went to see when they were finished, even though I love those buildings. They are three very decent works. One is the Iowa Laser Laboratory (1987–1992) in Iowa City. Another is the Herman Miller factory (1985–1989) in Rocklin, near Sacramento, California, and the third dates from before both of them, the Sirmai-Peterson house (1983–1988) in Thousand Oaks, also in California. In the case of the Sirmai-Peterson house, the clients became super-protective of their privacy and their place.

FORSTER They wouldn't let you in?

GEHRY They would have let me in, but you know, we sent Grant Mudford to photograph it, and he left his camera in the wrong place on the floor and they threw him out. They wouldn't let him finish. They loved me, they loved

Frank O. Gehry, Hermann Miller
Western Regional Facility, 1985–1989,
Rocklin, California

Frank O. Gehry, Sirmai-Peterson
Residence, 1983–1988,
Thousand Oaks, California

Frank O. Gehry, Guggenheim
Museum Bilbao, 1991–1997,
Bilbao, Spain

Frank O. Gehry, Guggenheim
Museum Bilbao, Atrium,
1991–1997, Bilbao, Spain

the house, they take care of it. I know, because I've seen pictures. It's
immaculate, but it's almost too much, so I couldn't go see it. I wasn't looking forward to the meeting, so I didn't go see it. With the Herman Miller
building, all the people that I worked with on the project wound up leaving
the company. So there was nobody to enjoy it with. I've never gone back.
The Iowa Laser Lab project got embroiled in politics having to do with the
University hiring three distinguished professors in the field, but in the end, it
didn't happen. So the building is not a laser lab, but rather something else,
and the people I worked with, the laser scientists, are not there. I have never
gone back.

FORSTER So these three buildings lie in the shadow of your relationship
with the client.

Frank O. Gehry, Guggenheim Museum Bilbao,
Interior, 1991–1997, Bilbao, Spain

Frank O. Gehry, Wosk Residence, Penthouse,
1981–1984, Beverly Hills, Los Angeles, California

141. GUGGENHEIM · BILBAO · F.GEHRY

Frank O. Gehry, Guggenheim Museum Bilbao, 1992

"The best work Frank did until now, are Bilbao and his house as it originally was." Robert Wilson

GEHRY   When I think about it, I realize that it's the process I really enjoy, the relationship. Maybe because I don't want to be alone out there, maybe because there is something really scary about being alone in the world. Maybe it's just my do-gooder instinct, I don't know. I don't know how much of this has to do with being the nice guy, wanting to be loved. There may be some negative stuff involved, but I enjoy working with people. I really enjoy the twists and turns the process takes when I can work with good clients, like Tom Krens and the Guggenheim in Bilbao. For me, that's really exciting, to see where it can go. The forms grow out of these relationships, and in the end, the clients become complicit. That's why I had a lot of fun with Miriam Wosk, who was doing those weird Art Deco things. They were not my cup of tea at all, but I really enjoyed working with her

"I miss not having had the chance to do an inaugural event with his Museum in Korea." Robert Wilson

BECHTLER   Were Hermann Finsterlin's fantastical visions ever an inspiration – for Bilbao?

GEHRY   No, I don't think so. For me, Eric Mendelsohn was more inspiring— not just because he was working in California, but because he had a strong vision of his own.

FORSTER   You give new impetus to a notion that was dominant for hundreds of years. In the Renaissance, buildings were thought to have two parents: the client who commissioned the building and the architect who designed it. Neither could do without the other in realizing a project. What you described is more interesting, though. The kind of joint authorship you are talking about changes the roles of client and architect. The client may give you a problem that allows you to pick up something that you might not have otherwise approached that way, and vice versa. By now your position is different from that of most architects. Clients come to you because they have something in mind that only you can create.

GEHRY   I know that it's true, but I don't accept it. I assume from the beginning that we're going to do something new, that it's going to come out of our relationship, and that it's not going to look like anything else I've done. And if they have a specific expectation, it can be undermined.

FORSTER You can undermine it, just as others would have to expect traditional demands.

GEHRY The criticism I've had from clients—well, Tom Krens even spelled it out in his text for the Venice Biennale exhibition. He wrote about his relationship with me, and was basically very positive, but he echoed a familiar critique: "Why do you keep changing this thing?" My only answer to that is that, when I meet with a client, and the client comes up with some new thing, I grab it and go with it.

"Tradition was his enemy. Throughout the architectural challenges he confronts, the concepts and results always are audacious and new." Robert Rauschenberg

FORSTER Run with it.

GEHRY I run with it. The next time I meet with the client, I will have changed the building. The client may be complicit, but he still won't understand why I'm changing the building. Krens loved that. He would throw stuff on the table and I was willing to pick it up and run with it.

FORSTER But by doing that, he upset the equation that was already in the process of being solved, right? And so, if you would come forward with another creature.....

GEHRY I don't balk at these things. In fact, it's fuel for the fire, I love it. But when it comes after the thing has crystallized, I don't know what to do.

FORSTER You mentioned Norton Simon and the house you did for him, that at a certain point, he suddenly put the lid on the project. Did you feel that you were being deprived of realizing the full potential of your idea? Or do you think that he was onto something?

GEHRY In the moment, I was upset. But then, he did a lot of upsetting things around that same time. Berta and I were getting married, and he waited until we were in Cuzco, on our way to Machu Picchu, to call and tell me that I was fired. On my honeymoon! It was cruel.

FORSTER Actually, cruelty was the trait that struck me from the very first time I met him. I froze inside with the sudden recognition that this was a man who could do anything.

GEHRY He was tough, and we definitely had it out a few times. I've never had it out with a client that way. We called each other names and spit and yelled. It was really important for me to go through that experience, because afterward, having survived it, we ended up being good friends until the end. I served on the board of his museum with his wife. She was involved in all this yelling and screaming and crying. She took his side, of course, whenever we would have a knock-down drag-out fight.

FORSTER Your relationship with clients is truly reciprocal. You don't play courtier to the prince, but instead dance with the client.

GEHRY Yes, even with Norton Simon. He toughened me up for the future, because having been through that, I could face anything.

FORSTER Who's going to frighten you after that?

GEHRY No one's going to frighten me like that. It was an experience to survive and come out the other end. In fact, a year or two before Norton died, when he was in a wheelchair, he called me. He wanted to build a new house. And he took me to a site up in the Hollywood hills and showed me a house, and asked what I thought of it. I said "You've got to tear it down." And he said "That's what I thought. But I like the site. Would you be willing to build a new house on it for me?" I said, "Norton, I would rather pay the psychiatrist's bill for you to go and discuss this with him, because you're absolutely crazy." I wouldn't do it. I said "I'm not going to fall into that trap again. You're crazy to even suggest it, because you can't build it." (He was sitting in a wheelchair at the time, couldn't move, breathing with an oxygen tank.) But I loved the chutzpah!

FORSTER You didn't believe that he would want to build another house in the condition he was in?

GEHRY I didn't want to go through it, because if he was cranky when he was whole and healthy.....

FORSTER Oh, he would have been insufferable if he wasn't!

GEHRY Can you imagine the tricks he would play, hiding behind the nurses and the sickness and the doctors, and....? Oh, I didn't want it. I said "I don't think you want it, I don't think you could survive it. Buy a house, and I'll help you find one you can move right into." Which is what he finally did.

Philip Johnson, Kunsthalle, 1963–1968, Bielefeld, Germany

FORSTER Norton Simon cannot have been your only difficult client.

GEHRY Oh, no. There's always Bielefeld.

FORSTER Frau Brigitte Oetker?

GEHRY She pointed to my model for the expansion of the Kunsthalle in Bielefeld (1994, unbuilt), and said, "This will soon be démodé," and then went to the press and insulted me in public.

FORSTER Why do you think she would do that?

GEHRY She vowed that the building would not be built. That she would not let it be built.

FORSTER Is she the principal donor for its construction?

GEHRY She said she was.

FORSTER This would have been the second instance of your following in Philip Johnson's footsteps, the first being the Winton guest house, since he had built the first building for the Kunsthalle in Bielefeld.

GEHRY Philip loved it.

"Frank was looking at a photograph of Einstein, that very much resembled himself, then he looked at me and said 'interesting'."
Robert Wilson

FORSTER Yes, I would think so. He probably wished he had done it himself.

GEHRY I didn't know anything about the Oetker family and their power.

FORSTER Yes. You might say the Oetkers are Bielefeld.

GEHRY I met with Dr. Weisner, the director of the museum. I asked him why he didn't want Philip to do it, and Weisner said, "Well, Johnson doesn't really want to do it." That wasn't true. Philip would have done it in a minute. Weisner may have had some vision of what I would do. So, I had three meetings with him. At the last meeting, he asked me if I would do the design gratis, because they didn't have any money. I said I'd love to do it for them, but I just couldn't. And he left it at that, saying he was going to go back and fund-raise. Then he died. I was sitting in the Aedes Gallery in Berlin and a German woman came over to me and said, "Herr Gehry?" "Yes," I answered. "I have something to show you," she said. And she gave me the newspaper, the obituary page, which had a big ad in one corner. "Dr. Ulrich Weisner has died," and then it listed all of his good works, and at the bottom, it was suggested: "Instead of flowers, send money to build the Frank Gehry addition to the museum."

FORSTER Actually, I've never heard of such a designation in an obituary notice.

GEHRY I was in shock: first that he had died; second that I appeared in an obituary column in this way. I found it very moving. Several weeks later, a businessman from Bielefeld came to see me, and he said "We want you to do the study," and he reminded me of the obituary column. And he added, "The board of the museum wants to realize Weisner's wishes, but we don't have any money, we have to raise the money. Would you make a model?" In the end, we made a deal that they would pay $100,000 for the model. We ended up spending twice as much as that to make it, of course. The date we were supposed to present it was set for a few days ago. Innocently, I went to Bielefeld. I was taken to a dinner in the Philip Johnson building. My two models were there already, one of the building alone, and another, a bigger model in wood showing the whole context of the site. There were about fifty people there. These people were very well dressed. They told me the Prime Minister, Johannes Rau, was there, but they didn't introduce me, they just said he would be there. Then they confessed that one unfortunate thing had happened: the Oetkers had called to say they couldn't make it. And this was very upsetting to everyone, that these people had reneged on their promise. I didn't know what was going on. I made my presentation. There was this woolly-looking man sitting in front who had wonderful eyes and was very expressive, and as I talked, he was very understanding. So I talked to him, I explained the project to him. If you do this kind of thing often, you wind up finding a friendly face and talking to that person. I looked around and talked to the others, but mostly I talked to this woolly man. Well, it turned out that he was Johannes Rau, but I had no idea.

FORSTER This is a wonderful example of your radar for clients.

GEHRY We made a terrific connection. My presentation wasn't stiff and stodgy. You know how I am. I got up and talked about Dr. Weisner, and I talked about what I felt about his realizing his dream. And I talked about Philip Johnson and my relationship with him, and about Richard Serra. I even talked about the bad things in my relationship with Serra. I was pretty open and frank about it. I was Frank. And I think that I really connected with these people. I said, "This thing looks like a meteorite that just blew in from Mars," but, I said, "Bear with me, because the model is an abstraction and in the end, it won't look like a meteorite. For instance, I started with a cube, which has a relationship to Johnson's glass house, a smaller cube, and I've added certain pieces, still keeping the scale in play with the existing building.

FORSTER It's the effect of the Shiva.

GEHRY Right, exactly! So, I said, "Understand that this is a very early design, and that it is based on three meetings with a client who no longer exists." Johannes Rau got up to speak, after me, and gave a wonderful talk. He understood. The next day, I had to make a presentation to the membership of the museum, which is now five hundred people instead of fifty. When the question period came, a little man put up his hand, said that he was from Bad Oeynhausen and that he had been a supporter of my work in the beginning, but now that he had seen the building built, he wanted to tell these people not to let me into Bielefeld, because I would destroy the town.

FORSTER What was his role in the project at Bad Oeynhausen?

GEHRY He was an engineer. A couple of days later, he was in Bad Oeynhausen, riding his bicycle up and down the street, stopping everyone who went into the building and telling them to hate it. I've never seen anything quite like it.

FORSTER We have been talking about your relationship to your clients, even though this last story leaves us on a rather uninspiring note. There have been others, to be sure. Even when there was no building, you have had

Frank O. Gehry/Philip Johnson, Lewis Residence,
1989–1995, Lyndhurst, Ohio

Frank O. Gehry/Philip Johnson, Lewis Residence,
1989–1995, Lyndhurst, Ohio

remarkable relationships with clients. The process was all-important in your
rapport with Peter Lewis, for example. One has the impression that the give
and take, the interaction, effectively replaced the customary product. Lewis
paid you even though he did not build the house you invented for him in
Cleveland (Peter B. Lewis house, unbuilt, 1989–1995). Basically, he paid for
having a relationship with you rather than for getting a house from you.

GEHRY Peter Lewis is a very complicated man, a brilliant businessman, but
not very visual. He probably never should have tried to have a house built,
probably never would have liked it, and probably never would have lived in
it. But he did like the interplay with me, and with the office. We had some
tough meetings and some happy meetings, but finally, everyone under-
stands that what Lewis did was to give me a five-year MacArthur to study
materials and form. And those investigations led to a lot of new projects.
Work that is being done now comes out of it—Bilbao, the Experience Music
Project (since 1996) in Seattle. Studies that were done as "research" during

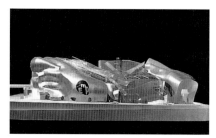

Frank O. Gehry, Experience Music Project, since
1996, Seattle Center Campus, Seattle, Washington

LOWIS . MAY 92

Frank O. Gehry, Lewis Residence, 1992

Frank O. Gehry, Lewis Residence, 1992

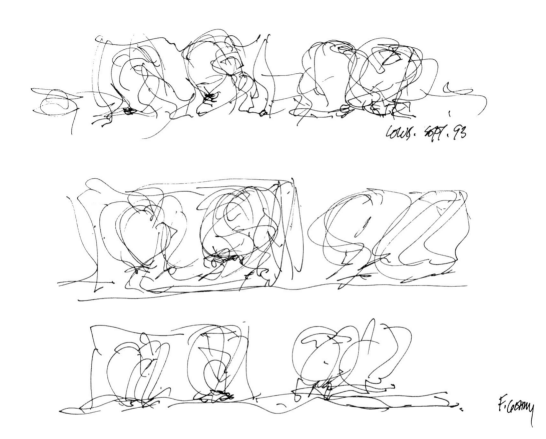

Frank O. Gehry, Lewis Residence, 1993

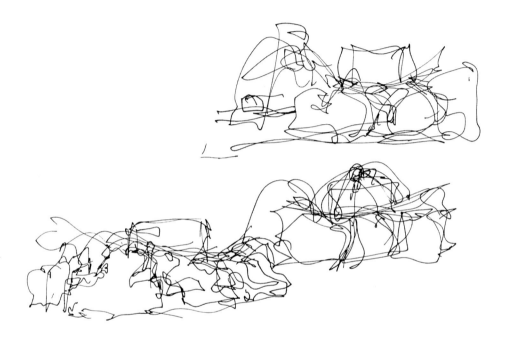

Dec.'96

Frank O. Gehry, Experience Music Project, 1996

Frank O. Gehry, Weatherhead School of Management,
Case Western Reserve University, Model, 1998, Cleveland, Ohio

that time and were paid for by Peter became the basis for my ongoing projects. After the house went away, he continued to keep in touch. And, when Case Western Reserve University in Cleveland decided to build a management school, Peter was approached. He made a substantial contribution because he had a relationship with Case Western, but also because he was given the right to choose the architect. He asked me to do it. We have been working on the Peter B. Lewis Campus of the Weatherhead School of Management (1996–1999), and I believe that this one is going to be built. So, there has been this fifteen-year relationship, which is friendly, and which has had quite a positive effect on my work.

Rudolf Schindler, Janson House,
1948/49, Hollywood Hills, Los Angeles,
California

Jasper Johns, Wilderness I,
1963–1970

Frank O. Gehry, Weatherhead School of Management, 1997

cx/t .97 – oct.

Frank O. Gehry, Weatherhead School of Management, 1997

Cross Westown. June/97

Frank O. Gehry, Weatherhead School of Management, 1997

FORSTER There are famous instances of a special client-architect relationship producing a building, but the relationship breaking up in the process. Remember Mies Van der Rohe and Dr. Farnsworth? It was Edith Farnsworth who made Mies say "The architect doesn't come with the house. You can have the child, but don't think I'm going to play wife." You haven't only had exceptional relationships with clients, but also with other architects and artists. When did these collaborations begin? Was Claes Oldenburg one of the first?

"I submitted a design for a gate-house to Lewis house at the entrance of the property. Frank seemed to think it was o.k., but the client wasn't moved enough." Frank Stella

GEHRY No. You know, I started out studying Fine Arts at USC, I studied ceramics with Glenn Lukens. Donald Goodall taught Art History, and I took his class and loved it. When I was a kid living in Toronto, my mother used to take me to the museum; she took me to concerts and she took me to look at art in the museum. I remember a crazy painting by John Marin hanging on the wall in this neoclassical atrium, and there was something very powerful about having this watercolor, this small thing suspended on the wall in such an important building.

FORSTER Did you see the larger Asian collection in the Royal Ontario Museum?

GEHRY Yes, but what I remember are the mummies.

FORSTER Of course, every school class probably went to see them.

GEHRY Going to the museum was what you did when we were kids. We used to go on our own to the theater and the museum.

FORSTER But that wouldn't necessarily lead to.....

GEHRY No, but then I went to college and started studying art history. Then there was Francis D'Erdly, with his cape. He did beautiful portraits, free ink studies. They were kind of Matisse with a Rouault brush, very expressive and powerful. And he cut quite a figure himself. He always smoked a cigarette the wrong way, like Europeans did, and he wore a cape, and all the girls followed him. I took his classes. Then Lukens, my ceramics teacher, was having a house built by Raphael Soriano, and he somehow realized that it would mean something to me to meet Soriano. So he introduced me, and I suddenly lit up.

FORSTER Oh, yes, I met him. In fact we published an interview with him in 1978 in the San Francisco magazine Archetype. We met up in Marin County.

GEHRY You went to the houseboat. I'd never seen a figure like that. He wore a black suit, black tie, black shirt, black beret, he looked like a pugilist, like he'd had his nose broken in a fight. Actually, a car had hit him. He walked around waving his arms and saying "Move this! Change that!" There was some kind of power in everything he did. I had just come from Canada, and I didn't know anything, and it was a bad time. My father had lost every- thing. I was really on the floor with lack of self-esteem. Not knowing what I wanted to do, when I was seventeen or eighteen, I had started working as a truck driver, and I was fascinated with people who did know what to do. I was looking for a model, I guess, and these guys fascinated me. My teacher, having seen me light up at the experience of seeing the house under con- struction, suggested that I take an architecture class. So I took a night class at USC. There were no other architecture schools out here; it was the only one, and it was a very expensive private school. I worked during the day and took night classes. I did really well. It was my first connection to some- thing. They skipped me to the second year. It was a big deal. Craig Kauff- man was in the class with me. He became an artist, a sculptor. Very flam- boyant character, very talented. Halfway through the second year, my teacher told me to get out of architecture, because I wasn't going to make it.

FORSTER Do you remember what it was that he found off-putting?

GEHRY Yes. He didn't think my drawings had any feeling. I remember it was when we were doing a project for a high school gymnasium. There was something about it he didn't like, and he called me in. Now this guy was Bill Schoenfeld who became the architect for the Los Angeles County Airport, a job he had for many years. He only just retired. I've seen him, and he remembers the story and says he was wrong. At the time, though, I had enough horsepower in my head to go beyond him. I just said "I don't care. This is what I like and I'm going to do it." Subsequently I did better, but hav- ing come from the Fine Arts, I was always trying to put architects together with artists at school. And I used to go to Goodall, who was the dean, and concoct projects between the architecture and art departments. But I always failed. They would never cooperate. The artists and the architects were in the same building, but never talked.

FORSTER Particularly in those years. That was one of the worst moments with regard to any connection among the different arts.

GEHRY No one would deal with it. I was this weirdo who was trying to do something in common.

FORSTER By that time you must have decided that ceramics wasn't really your métier.

GEHRY I quit studio art. I was in architecture, and I was doing well.

FORSTER When you went to Harvard, you transferred to a school that was even less inclined toward collaboration between artists and architects.

GEHRY Yes, but what happened was that my liberal Jewish upbringing was activated. It was the McCarthy era and I got into all kinds of trouble. I joined funny organizations. I had been influenced by Gregory Ains and Garrett Eckbo at USC. There was a lot of anxiety. The FBI planted informants in our classes. We discovered one, a guy who was reporting on people's activities. McCarthyism was real.

FORSTER Nothing to joke about.

GEHRY I studied city planning, drawn in by the idea that you could plan the bigger picture of the city. I thought this was liberal and reasonable. We didn't want to do window detailing. I remember we used to curse "window details for rich people's houses." No, we wanted to change the world. Our professors were suggesting that it was possible.

FORSTER Was that what led you to Harvard?

GEHRY José Luis Sert represented urban design, bringing the largest scale to bear on the city. I applied to Harvard thinking that I would go into city planning because of Sert. When I got there, I realized it was Reginald Isaacs, and that meant government bureaucracy. I was in the wrong pew, but it was too late. I went to see Sert and asked to transfer to his department, but he wouldn't let me. He was really nasty, and I never forgave him for it. I know Frankie Sert, his nephew, who took the title of Conde from Sert, who had rejected it in protest of Franco's regime. That had also appealed to me. When I got to Harvard and he rejected me, there I was with two daughters and no money, I had just gotten out of the Army, and I arrived at this place, bright-eyed and bushy-tailed, twenty-five years old. I wanted to study with my models, but I realized I was in the wrong place. So Sert said to me, "You're a young man. Go home, reapply, and then come back to the school," and I said "Give me a break. I'm not going to reapply. There's not much likelihood that I can afford to reapply." So I was stuck. While I was in the planning school, there was a charrette for one of Sert's projects, a secret project. He invited students, and I was included. I could draw pretty well, so they found me and asked me if I would participate in the charrette. I ended up going, but then I found out what the secret project was: a palace for Batista. Well, I was furious.

"On a scale of 100, Bilbao on the outside would get a 125, inside 85, and the Exhibition a 75." Walter De Maria

FORSTER There goes another title.

GEHRY So that was the second strike against it. In the space of a week, I walked out. I was so discouraged. By then, I should have known better. When Sert came out to Los Angeles to do fundraising, long after I'd finished school, they called me to a meeting where I found myself sitting next to him. He knew by then that I was interested in art. I was connected to Oldenburg and Rauschenberg and all those people, and he knew it. He was looking for help with the Carpenter Center. And I told him, "You've got all the wrong artists there." And that's when he told me, "Well, the artists that you hang out with are démodé." Now, he didn't use that exact term, but that's what he meant. He said "This is just a flash in the pan. You know, Tino Nivola is a great artist." Well, I loved Nivola. When I was at school, he was one of my favorite people, but a great artist he wasn't.

FORSTER In his own practice, Sert represented precisely that split between architecture and art, where the only vestiges of artistic practice that had survived in architecture were bright colors on balconies or some such thing. So, one is interested in how you established your relationships with artists. How did you come to know Oldenburg?

GEHRY When I went to Harvard, the world of Le Corbusier first opened up for me. I had come from Los Angeles, and the only architecture I saw when I got out of USC was influenced by the Japanese beetle-bug language. I just wasn't interested in Le Corbusier. But then at Harvard, my eyes were opened to European architecture. I hadn't been to Europe yet, but Sigfried Giedion, Jacob Bakema, Eduard Sekler, were all at Harvard at the time. I was just an auditor, not a registered student in the architecture department, so I had to hide out in the back of the room. I never really knew Sekler until recently. When I met him, I told him I used to mooch on his lectures at Harvard. I reminded him about some of those lectures, and he realized that I had in fact been there. He gave one of the great lectures on the Golden Mean. Jacques Michel was in the design studio and I got to know him. He had worked with Corbusier on Ronchamp for several years. In fact, he made all the models. All those beautiful little models. We became friends because I had worked for Victor Gruen who also was at Harvard then.

"It is clearly the case that at the moment Frank's sculptural forms are seen only as critique—indeed as humor, criticism at its most threatening—by many who feel that the preservation of this idea of a teleological imperative of a certain sort should be the main concern of any culture. Witness the silliness which caused his proposal for Berlin's museum island to be rejected. So yes, I think Gehry does change the sacred neutral space of the museum, by taking the same attitude towards it that artists do."
Jeremy Gilbert-Rolfe

FORSTER Essentially, you got in touch with much more of the European tradition than Harvard itself had to offer.

GEHRY They had a fake representative of it. I had a terrible time with Charlie Eliot III, who descended from the family of the great reformers of Harvard. He was head of one of the sections of the Planning Department. He embarrassed me one day in front of Sert, saying some terrible things about what I was doing, because I was trying to make urban planning into three-dimensional architecture.

FORSTER Wasn't that what everyone was beginning to do?

GEHRY Well, they just wouldn't have it. Because I was trying to solve all the problems that they gave us to solve, I bit off more than I could chew. I arrived at the crit and wasn't all together. So they massacred me. Sert was there and didn't defend me. I felt.....

FORSTER Twice sold down the river?

GEHRY Yes, Sert sold me down the river. I remember that afterward, I ran back to Robinson Hall to see Charlie Eliot. He was standing on this kind of ship's ladder that went up to his office. I swung open the door. He stood there like Charles Laughton (he actually looked like Charles Laughton), glaring down at me, and said "Yes?" And I said "I'm finished!" And WHAM! I left. I never went back. I read later that George Santayana had the same problem with Charlie's grandfather. So it felt like I was in good company.

FORSTER Maybe it was even more complicated because you were treading on terrain where you couldn't yet stand.

GEHRY I thought I was a failure, so I quit. But what to do with the rest of my school term? That's when I started going to hear lectures on just about anything. And my liberal Jewish political mentality was really exercised by some of them. J. Robert Oppenheimer gave a major series of lectures and I attended all of them. I was bowled over. Then there was a debate between Norman Thomas and Howard Fast. Howard Fast was the writer who wrote Citizen Tom Paine and Spartacus. He debated Thomas and lost. Somehow it was pathetic. I subsequently met him at a dinner party at a film star's house. This was many years later, when he had become a screen writer. I was sitting next to him, and I asked him.....

FORSTER How it felt?

GEHRY No, I asked him what happened after that. This was twenty-five years later. And I said "Where did you go? You disappeared into the movies?" And he said "That man destroyed me," he said "I've never been the same." He admitted it to me. He said "I quit everything. I copped out, became a screenwriter, just decided to make money. He destroyed my will." He said "He made me realize how shallow my do-gooder bullshit was. I couldn't stand up to this guy." He said, "I realized how shallow I was," or something like that.

FORSTER Incredible.

GEHRY I haven't seen him since. Margaret Mead also taught at Harvard at that time, Hugh Gaiteskell, Barbara Ward, John Kenneth Galbraith, Arthur Schlesinger, Jr., and Pitirim Sorokin were all teaching there.

FORSTER So in a sense, it is by opting out of planning that all of these other things suddenly opened up for you. I was wondering how you did it, because students of architecture and planning have very little time. They don't usually wander around the university listening to every interesting speaker. Did you ever go down to New York during that time?

GEHRY Yes, but I had a wife and kids, and no money. We were living on the GI Bill. I worked at Harvard, too. There was Hideo Sasaki, then Perry, Shaw, Hepburn & Dean—they were the guys who restored Williamsburg, and I worked on the tail end of that. And I took a class with Joseph Hudnut.

FORSTER You did? You probably read his book, Architecture and the Spirit of Man.

GEHRY Yes, that was the first time I ever heard the word postmodern. He gave a lecture where he used the term in 1946 or 1947, and then there it was again in an article he wrote on the postmodern house. He was teaching at M.I.T. He would take us on walks through Boston and talked about "American" architecture. And that was when it really hit me.

BECHTLER In connection with the concept of post-modernism, when did you first hear about Josef Plečnik?

GEHRY Well, it wasn't while I was at Harvard. I don't recall the exact moment, but when I did become aware of Plečnik, I was very interested. About fifteen years ago, I took a trip to Vienna and saw his Crypt in the Church of the Holy Spirit (1910–1913), which was very impressive.

FORSTER You hadn't seen any "American" architecture out in California?

GEHRY No. But Hudnut talked about it, and that made a big impression on me and gave me something to strive for: creating an American architecture. After all, I was in America, I should make American architecture. And that meant that you had to find a new language, because one didn't really exist yet. It existed in the way he explained it, but the game was to find a new one. How do you do something when nobody is doing it yet?

FORSTER What did he talk about? The Boston Customs House and things of this nature?

GEHRY No, he took us to look at the row houses.

FORSTER The row houses?

GEHRY Lewisburg Square. He talked about industrial buildings, took us to the industrial section. That was the beginning.

FORSTER That's interesting. Around that time John Coolidge was also teaching at Harvard. He wrote The Mill and the Mansion, a book about industrial architecture in Massachusetts. In the midst of the McCarthy era, with this particular taste in your mouth, you fixated on creating an architecture that you defined using the adjective "American." Why would you have wanted to do that?

GEHRY I was optimistic about America. It made me more American to fight McCarthy. And the people I was hanging around with were all optimistic. We were going to find a new way. It was all about finding new ways.

FORSTER But, in finding new ways, did you relate to the way painters and sculptors were already trying to make an American art?

"One of his greatest achievements is to collect the history of contemporary art and with an unabashed exuberance, wit, cunning and playfulness make it his own vocabulary." Richard Serra

GEHRY When I got back from Harvard, I went to work for William Pereira for a while on the airport project in Los Angeles, but it didn't work out. I also worked on the "saucer restaurant" there.

FORSTER You worked on that piece of space-age kitsch?

GEHRY Yes, and then I went to work for Victor Gruen, where I met a graphics designer, Marion Sampler. He was head of graphics at Gruen's office, but was also a painter. We started going to galleries together. That's how I met Rolf Nelson, who later married my sister. Rolf had a gallery. He used to show Judy Chicago and other artists, and we became friends. Irving Blum had a gallery on La Cienega, near Rolf's, so we used to go gallery hopping, and we met all the artists. I bought some works by Judy. I loved being around artists, and I felt quite close to them. I met Kenneth Price and Ed Moses. Moses tried to hire me to do a garage remodel for him. I met him when I did the Danziger studio (1964). While the building was under construction, I saw this crazy guy standing on the building site. It was Moses. And then, every time I would go over there, someone else would be hanging around. Moses spread the word that this building was going up, and that it was different. That was how I met Ken Price, and Billy Al Bengston came to see it, too. I met a lot of artists around this time because they came to look at my building under construction, and I knew who they were, and I was very excited about meeting them. I was very excited that they were interested in what I was doing, and I took a big interest in what they were doing.

FORSTER A real coterie?

GEHRY I was invited to their studios. There were about ten artists, Robert Irwin, John Altoon, Babs Altoon (John's wife at the time). Through Altoon and Babs I met Jasper Johns. Jasper used to come to town and we'd have dinner with him, and we became friends. I met the Grinsteins and the Gemini people.

FORSTER And you did the gallery for Gemini G.E.L. (1976–1979).

GEHRY That was when I met Rauschenberg. He and I became really good friends. I used to go to New York and drink with him. We're talking about the early to mid-1960s. I had a client in New York from the beginning, David Rosen, who was involved in city planning projects in upstate New York, and he used to invite me to New York to do the drawings with him. I'd met him at Gruen's office. He was also interested in art, so I would go to New York and work for him for a week or two at a time, and we would hang out at Max's Kansas City in Soho.

Larry Bell was very hot at the time. He was in New York a lot and he and I used to hang out, and I also became good friends with John Chamberlain. At the time, he was living with Ultra Violet and he used to drag me to The Factory with Andy Warhol, where I met Viva and Paul Morrisey. Chamberlain and I have stayed friends all these years. During that period, I was dating. I had left my wife, and I was dating a girl that worked for me, a Chinese girl, Vivienne Kauffman, who was Craig's ex-wife. Vivienne was a friend of Oldenburg's, and she was sewing his "Fagends" at the time.

FORSTER So this is how you met Oldenburg, through a woman who was sewing his cigarette butts?

GEHRY Claes had done the drawing for "The Passing of the Izuma." He said he was looking for an architect to do working drawings for the "Tobacco Can," because it was meant to be a real building. I saw him a few times, but he never did call me back. I went to New York, had dinner at his house, and met his wife Patty.

FORSTER Another seamstress.

GEHRY Yes, she used to sew all of his stuff. At that time I guess I met James Rosenquist, Tom Wesselman, Kynaston McShine. Warhol was hanging around with Edie Sedgwick. We all used to go to Small's Paradise in Harlem.

FORSTER An interesting aspect about your friendship with Chamberlain is that you used to do a lot with car bumpers.

GEHRY I actually designed a building in Hollywood for a chrome plating factory where they did bumpers, the Faith Plating Company (1964/65). I was into that sort of thing. Chamberlain was accessible as a person, easy to get on with, easy to talk to. I haven't seen much of him lately, but I consider him a really good old friend. But the artists whose work I loved most were Don Judd, Carl Andre, and the Minimalists.

"Bilbao looks as though it would make a damn fine cathedral, like San Marco in Venice." Carl Andre

FORSTER What interested you in Andre?

GEHRY Actually, I couldn't figure that out either. I'll tell you how it happened. There was a show at the Jewish Museum in New York, in 1966, called "Primary Structures: Younger American and British Sculptors."

FORSTER That was a landmark show.

GEHRY Judy Chicago and a lot of my other friends from out on the West Coast were included, even DeWain Valentine. I went to see the show, and I remember there was a Ron Bladen. And then there was this row of bricks. This double row of firebricks. And I remember we'd had a lot to drink, and I was walking through and I tripped over some of the bricks, and I thought, "Now why have they got firebricks here?" And so I followed the line to the wall and the label said "Carl Andre," something like "One hundred and something firebricks." And afterwards we went to Small's Paradise with Warhol and Sedgwick and the whole group. Finally I went back to the hotel, but I couldn't forget those bloody firebricks, and I kept wondering why were they there and what this Andre guy was all about. At the same time, I was starting to work with chain-link, and I was fascinated. I was looking for an architecture that you could dial up, phone in. You could call somebody and describe the coordinates, and they could build the thing. That was a fantasy. But here were these firebricks, and I thought, this artist is smart. He doesn't even come to the gallery. He gives them a coordinate on the wall, he calls the brickyard and says "Put in a hundred and whatever firebricks, two layers, soldier course, perpendicular to the wall." I thought that was amazing. And I fantasized about it for a few weeks. And then I came back to Los Angeles, and of course we had many evenings with Price and Moses, and so they took me to a dinner with Andre at the Grinstein's house. So finally I met him, and I said "Man, you are doing stuff that really interests me, because you could just call the thing up." He just looked at me.

FORSTER Was he offended?

GEHRY Yeah! He said, "That's not what it's about!" I said "What do you mean? What is it about?" He said "Let me tell you something." And he started drawing. I still have the drawing. He said "When you say 155 bricks, it's over just like that. But think about it this way: firebrick, firebrick, firebrick, firebrick, firebrick, firebrick, firebrick." He said "It's the tactile thing of setting them up. I put those firebricks there. I enjoyed doing that. That's what my kicks are, to buy the firebricks, load them in the truck, take them to the gallery, and set them up." So it's a tactile thing. He made these drawings and then gave them to Ken Price. And I said, "I'm the one who asked you! How can you give him the drawings?" A few weeks later, one of the drawings was framed, and Price gave it to me as a gift when I saw him at a dinner. I've always been fascinated with Andre.

FORSTER Were you swayed by this explanation?

GEHRY Yeah, I bought it! It made me think about the experience of working with materials. It sort of fit.

"Frank's house was very groovy, Californian-dreaming and I thought the Beach Boys would have been very comfortable in his house."
Frank Stella

FORSTER But the "phone-in" concept could get quite transcendent.

GEHRY I was more interested in that at the time. And anyway, who was doing architecture in Los Angeles in the 1960s? There was John Lautner, who was cranky, and you couldn't get near him. And besides, he was basically doing Frank Lloyd Wright stuff, which by then had started to wane for me. Ray Kappe was friendly, but rather distant. Bernard Zimmermann was a star at the time. He was very cranky about my work, and especially the Danziger studio and residence: "How could somebody do windows like that? What a stupid thing that was." So the architecture milieu was not accessible to me. Schindler was gone; I met Richard Neutra a few times, but I didn't find him very exciting to be around. There was a young group of people around Neutra and Robert Alexander who were very involved in all the lefty organizations I belonged to, as were Gregory Ain and Garrett

Eckbo. Social planning interested me, but architecture didn't. And there was no connection between that and art. I had become part of the art scene and it was the artists who were very supportive of my work from the beginning. To this day, Jasper Johns still comes to my exhibitions. He came to one of my shows in New York and bought a fish lamp. I always loved Serra's work, but I didn't know him. When I built my house in 1978, the Grinsteins brought Philip Glass and Richard Serra over to see it.

FORSTER The two of them together?

"The structure spanned the skyline of Manhattan puncturing the Chrysler Building, which also functioned as its midway support. At the time people called it utopian, Frank and I considered it to be practical. This was one of the first examples of Frank using a fish to define structure." Richard Serra

GEHRY Yes. And they wandered around and then Serra came to see me. I met Philip Johnson when I did the Ron Davis house (1968–1972) in Malibu, because he was interested in it.

BECHTLER That was before your first colaboration with Richard Serra in 1981 for the project in New York, that would have connected a huge fish sculpture installed in the middle of the Hudson River with steel armature suspended from the Queensborough Bridge.

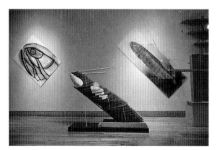

Frank O. Gehry with Richard Serra,
Bridge Project for New York, 1981, New York

Frank O. Gehry, Bentwood Furniture
Studies, 1989–1992

Frank O. Gehry with Prototype Chairs for Knoll Int.,
1991

"We were asked to make a proposal for a footbridge across the Thames, connecting St. Paul's cathedral with the New Tate. We decided that the main purpose of a footbridge across the Thames shouldn't only be to transport people from point A to point B. We proposed instead a bridge where sociality was to be the dominant practical purpose." Richard Serra

GEHRY Yes, this was my first collaboration with Richard. He urged me to go all the way with the fish, because I would have been too timid about it. So I decided to make it out of glass. It eventually developed into a glass wall system. I wish I could have built it.

BECHTLER But the fish project wasn't your only attempt at doing a bridge, was it? In 1996, you collaborated with Serra again, on a submission for the competition to design the Millennium Bridge across the Thames River in London.

"We curved the span of the bridge towards the New Tate and ended the walkway of the bridge in a large-scale plaza above the Thames which would permit for cultural and public events of all kinds." Richard Serra

GEHRY I got into that one at the last minute. Richard Serra had been invited to submit a scheme, and I had just twenty-four hours to concoct something. We worked with the engineer Jörg Schlaich, who invented a system of trusses for our bridge. The whole thing was accomplished in a flurry of telephone calls and faxes. But you know the result: the jury didn't like our project.

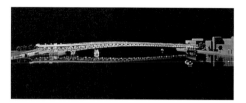

Frank O. Gehry, with Richard Serra, Millennium Bridge, Project, 1996, London

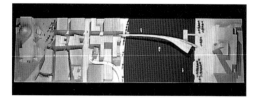

Frank O. Gehry, with Richard Serra, Millennium Bridge, Project, 1996, London

FORSTER Would you go back for a moment to the late 1970s? Serra was a different Serra at that time. He made weight and pressure work as sculptural qualities, using sheets of lead and steel. There seemed to be something threatening in the material and in the way it had been propped up. Just as the composer Philip Glass had not yet begun to practice his lush repetitiveness, but made leaner and more brittle music. How did Serra and Glass react when they saw your house?

"The footbridge we designed was not purely an engineering feat but an enormous cantilevered pier fronting the Tate. Our bridge was a hybrid. We lost the competition to a structure that reflected the worst of mediocre modernism." Richard Serra

GEHRY They came to see it. They loved it. They were very supportive, and this clinched it for me. I was in.

FORSTER One could turn around and say that your house became something of a permanent exhibit.

"We consciously tried to create a form whose reading would extend into the realm of the imagination." Richard Serra

GEHRY Oldenburg came to the house with Coosje van Bruggen. That was the first time I met her, and in fact, the first time I met Oldenburg on an equal footing. Up until then, he was the master and I was an unknown. But all of a sudden, the house happened, and I got a call from them. That was sometime in 1982. It was raining that night. I'll never forget how he walked into the room and looked out the window, and the cactus in the yard was all wet. It looked like a metal sculpture, and he asked "How did you...when did you do that?" We spent a wonderful evening together. It was our first meeting on an equal basis, and he invited me to New York. In 1983, Claes gave me his original drawings for the Pasadena Museum, and he and Coosje asked me if they could come and spend time in my office, because they were just starting their large scale projects and didn't know how to build them, how to do them. Claes and Coosje came and lived in my office for two weeks. He watched me a lot, and then he made some beautiful little paper bag structures and houses, but someone stole all of them. That was the beginning of a long friendship. Our first collaboration was the project for a camp for kids who had cancer, Camp Good Times (1984/85) in the Santa Monica Mountains. Dustin Hoffman, the client, canceled the project because he thought kids with cancer wouldn't like it. "They like Huckleberry Finn," he said.

"The image of the bridge facilitated metaphorical transformations into an oar, a stem, a stringed instrument, a reptile, a ship."
Richard Serra

FORSTER Wasn't Il Corso del Coltello (1985) the big collaboration you, Oldenburg, and Van Bruggen worked on?
GEHRY That's right. After they had concocted their idea for the Corso del Coltello, they asked me to get involved, and Germano Celant, who was excited about my house, arranged for us to give a lecture at the Polytechnic University in Milan. It was a large class, and we had a lot of fun. We decid-

Frank O. Gehry, Summer Camp Good Times,
Model, 1984/85

Frank O. Gehry, Chiat/Day/Mojo,
1975/1989–1991, Venice, California

ed to make a project with the students, a floating city, Coltello Island. It was to be sited behind the Arsenale toward the cemetery, between where the vaporetto goes up the back end, on the way to the airport, and the Lagoon of the Dead. Oldenburg designed a theater library for Venice in the form of a pair of binoculars. I made a fire station out of a snake. We talked about an architecture of cutting and slicing. We developed this fantasy about buildings being sliced into pieces, then moving the slices around. This fit very well with the Swiss Army Knife, the Coltello/Ship in Three Stages (1984). I had a little model Claes had made for the library, a pair of red binoculars. It was always sitting on my desk after that. When I started to work on offices for the Chiat/Day/Mojo advertising agency (1989–1991) in Venice something happened. I was working on the idea of a tripartite facade. I had designed one part as trees, one as a boat, but the middle part remained a blank. We had a meeting with our client, Jay Chiat, a lunch meeting in my office, and he said "When are you going to finish the middle?" And I said "Jay, I always leave the best part for the end. Anyway, I don't know what I'm going to do." He said, "Well, tell me. I need to know where we're going with this." And I said, "Well, I want to do something in brick, towers, you know, like a castle gate, but not exactly a castle." I was sitting there grasping for words and Oldenburg's red binoculars were standing there in front of me on my desk. I don't know what got into me, but I picked them up and put them down in the middle, between the other two facades, and everybody gasped.

FORSTER As if you had premeditated a coup-de-theatre!

GEHRY It was just amazing. I said "Isn't that something. That really is perfect." So, Jay said, "Well, you know Oldenburg. Ask him to do it." I said, "Jay, Oldenburg doesn't work like that. This is too serendipitous, he would come and want to do something totally different." But Jay was very persuasive. So I called Oldenburg, and I said, "We've been working together on projects, like Camp Good Times. And remember when you made the red binoculars?" Then I just kept going, "I just did something with your binoculars. I know it's serendipitous, but before you say no, would you at least listen to me? And would you keep an open mind and come and see what I'm talking about? I'll send you pictures. You can change the binoculars, if you like, but it's just so perfect." So I sent the pictures and there was a week of silence. And finally the call came: "I like it. I like it. I like it. I need to work on it, but I like it." "You know," I said, "That's all I need to know, that you want to play." Then he started to work, turning the binoculars from this very rigid kind of thing into the most sensuous object. I have the model at home, I'm afraid to leave it around here. But when he came out to Los Angeles and made these beautiful, sensuous black binoculars, I started to get worried. Oldenburg was really pushing me, in terms of the other two pieces of the project, to keep up, to hold the stage with him. I remember saying to Chiat, "I don't know if my ego can stand this. I know that once we build this, there's going to be some magazine cover with a picture of the binoculars and my building will get cut out. You're asking a lot of me to go along with this. I'm a little worried about it." We continued anyway, and I began to enjoy what we were doing.

"I don't see any special reason why one, least of all Frank, should suppose that the fish form came before the force, that it wasn't liquidity and the idea of functioning within it that was attractive in the first place. This could be a direction one might take were one to ask what the fish was before it was a fish." Jeremy Gilbert-Rolfe

But in the process of working with Claes and Coosje, it became clear that they didn't have experience building buildings, and it was clear that I was a fish out of water making sculpture. But we talked a lot to one another about it and agonized about it and all that. I finally ended up saying that this was a building, so they had to become architects. But to be architects, they had to put a window in the building. Basically, I forced a window on them. And they struggled with that window as I knew they would, and as I have struggled with windows in my other buildings. They made slots that were hidden by the barrels of the binoculars. I think they kind of copped out, but they got the window in. It is hard. That's the fun of it. The interesting thing is the dividing line between the things we do, which is a very minor issue, because in the end, if they faced that window problem a few more times, it would simply become part of their language like everything else. It's easier to build sculpture because everything architectural is, by definition, sculptural, because first of all, it's three-dimensional. But I have trouble with god damned windows, too.

But then it happened. Sure enough, a magazine came out with the binoculars on the cover. Charles Jencks did it the first time. Then there was also a book. And, you know what? I didn't even notice! I said, "Gee, isn't it great, the binoculars building is published?" It was a while before I realized that my wildest fear had come true. When the Chiat/Day/Mojo building was finished, there were conferences about artist-architect collaborations, and at one of them, someone said "This is like the pig and the chicken walking down the street. They go up to the restaurant and see a sign that says "HAM & EGGS" The chicken is the architect and the artist is the pig." And then Mary Miss gave a talk here at UCLA where she said "The difference between art and architecture is that architects have to put toilets in their projects."

FORSTER But you know, Frank, she was just quoting Marcel Duchamp!

GEHRY Everyone worries about the artist's role being an afterthought of the architect. Now here was a situation where the artist was given front and center stage by the architect. Even I call it the "binoculars building." What happened was really interesting. Every architecture magazine and the popular press published that building. It certainly got published, but no art magazine reported on it. No Artforum, Art News, Art in America. Nothing.

FORSTER The Chiat/Day/Mojo project had been ten years in the making. It existed only as a model for so long, maybe as art, it felt a little passé?

GEHRY Maybe. But I was puzzled by it. And Jay Chiat was puzzled by it, because he is a big art collector and he hangs out with artists and collectors. He happened to know the editor of Art in America and asked him why they weren't interested. And the guy said "Oh, it's an oversight. Of course we're interested. We'll get on it right away." Well, of course they never did. It's never been done. I never could figure it out. Last year, Christopher Knight did an article on sculpture in public places. It was in the calendar section of the Los Angeles Times, and on the cover was a picture of Borofsky's "Clown," which is installed right across the street from the binoculars building. He talked about six or eight projects in Los Angeles, collaborations between artists and architects. The article was interesting. But he never mentioned the binoculars building. So I called him and said "Christopher, I don't need more press, but I just wondered, how come you didn't think of the Chiat/Day/Mojo building, when it's right across the road from the Borofsky? I'm just curious about what went through your mind, why you edited it out." There was silence. When I said "Well, maybe you don't like Oldenburg?" He said he loved the building, really loved it. So, I said, "Well, why then?" He said "I don't have an answer. I don't know. Let me think about it."

FORSTER Has he ever told you?

GEHRY No.

FORSTER Well, I have an answer. The answer may be that, unless someone knew how this building came about, who would suspect that the binoculars have a different origin from the rest of it? The amazing thing is that this building is made of three very distinct elements that nonetheless hang together. Once the binoculars had been inserted between "the boat" and "the trees", it all fell into place. You would never suspect that anybody else was involved. After all, you were struggling with the project until you reached for that memorable pair of binoculars on your desk. Kind of a surrealist act of automatic design. I think everyone looks at it as architecture, and in fact, it is architecture, full of associations with turrets and gateways. One doesn't think of it as a separate piece of sculpture.

GEHRY I did what I always did. I picked it off the shelf and co-opted it.

FORSTER Inside and out, this building covers many regions of the mind. The topography of its character is vast and diverse. I don't know how far we want to go into psychology, but at the beginning, you were feeling slightly squeamish about being the little boy under the shadow of the big

Frank Stella, Museum Hoffmann, Project,
1990–1993, Dresden, Germany

artist. In the end, you turned the tables right around. The artist disappeared
into an ensemble everybody thinks is just architecture.

GEHRY Maybe that's why I call it the binoculars building.

FORSTER There's one point that interests me in its broader implications.
You might say that there's been a possibility for collaboration between
architects and artists either when their respective fields are clearly demar-
cated, or when they tend to merge. In neoclassical architecture, you can fill
empty fields with sculpture, you can attach any number of ornamental elements. The opposite is the case with the baroque. With Borromini's buildings, it is completely arbitrary and beside the point to distinguish where the
wall ceases to be a wall and becomes a sculptural volume, a leg, swelling
curtains blown apart, a rock, a piece of velvet, or whatever. Ideally, in the
first case, you have two different artistic personalities; in the latter, you have
only one, who is an architect or a sculptor by degree. When you look at
yourself, you resemble in a sense the Baroque artist rather than the classi-
cist. Your relationship with Frank Stella is a classic illustration of this.

**"Bauhaus was formful as functional. The outside revealed the
inside. With a fish and an orange the skin is very different than
the interior."** Robert Wilson

Richard Meier will design a building as a container for art, and there can be
one Stella there in its sharply circumscribed place in the building. The affinity you were talking about between Stella's work and your own is of a different order. You look at Stella as if it were a kind of architecture in formation,
architecture becoming a sculpture.

"I don't know what sculpted architecture is. Richard Meier recently cast his wooden models in stainless steel. Perhaps Gehry will cast real museums in titanium. I have never seen a sacred neutral space in a museum building." Frank Stella

GEHRY I've obviously looked at his work a lot. And I've considered him an important source of information. But he was more accessible to me when I didn't know him. He got in touch with me when I was doing the cardboard furniture, and I showed him all the technical stuff. He came to see my house one night and just sat there looking. He didn't say much, and I didn't know whether he liked it or not. The first time I knew he liked it was several years later when he was giving a televised tour through his show at the Fogg Museum. He stopped in front of a painting and started talking about my work in relation to his paintings. He came to see me two years ago and showed me the project for the Kunsthalle in Dresden, and said, "It comes from you, Frank." I said "No, it's you," but it just happened that I was making shapes that looked like they came from him. Until I saw what he was doing, there was no other architect working in a language that had anything in common with mine.

"The first work of Frank that I saw was his house in Santa Monica, in the seventies. It wasn't that he was reckless, rather he was fearless as he went about cutting and tearing his house apart, and simultaneously reconstructing the shattered remains with mundane industrial materials. – This was innovation. It immediately impelled me to reconsider the house as a container."
Richard Serra

FORSTER Since so much of what you have been saying revolves around relationships and exchanges and sympathies between art and architectural practice, one could imagine that the museum might become the ideal arena for these collaborations.

GEHRY Yes, but as a building type, the art museum has sort of eluded me so far. I wish I had done more than just a few galleries and exhibition installations.

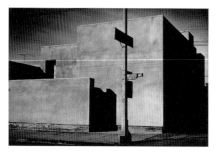

Frank O. Gehry, Danziger Studio-Residence,
1964/65, Hollywood, Los Angeles, California

Frank O. Gehry, Gemini G.E.L.,
1976–1979, Los Angeles, California

Frank O. Gehry, Art Treasures of Japan, 1965,
Los Angeles County Museum of Art, California

Frank O. Gehry, Art Treasures of Japan, 1965,
Los Angeles County Museum of Art, California

Frank O. Gehry, Gemini G.E.L.,
1976–1979, Los Angeles,
California

Frank O. Gehry, Art Treasures of Japan, 1965,
Los Angeles County Museum of Art, California

Frank O. Gehry, Avant-Garde in Russia 1910–1930, 1980, Los Angeles County Museum of Art, Los Angeles, California

Frank O. Gehry, Avant-Garde in Russia 1910–1930, 1980, Los Angeles County Museum of Art, Los Angeles, California

Frank O. Gehry, German Expressionist Sculpture, 1983, Los Angeles County Museum of Art, Los Angeles, California

Frank O. Gehry, German Expressionist Sculpture, 1983, Los Angeles County Museum of Art, Los Angeles, California

FORSTER You have built studios for artists. The Danziger studio, the Gemini G.E.L. building, and of course houses for artists like Ron Davis, and the gallery for Norton Simon's Malibu guest house. And let's not forget your exhibition installations, which span many years.

GEHRY The first exhibition design we did was for the Los Angeles County Museum, the "Art Treasures from Japan" show in 1965, the "Assyrian Reliefs" in 1966, the Norton Simon sculpture installation in 1967, and the Billy Al Bengston show in 1968.

FORSTER At LACMA, you also did "Avant-Garde in Russia 1910–1930" in 1980, "Seventeen Artists in the Sixties" in 1981, "German Expressionist Sculpture" in 1983.

GEHRY Somewhere in there we did the King Tut show, the "Treasures of Tutankhamen" (1978).

FORSTER King Tut?

GEHRY You didn't know that?

FORSTER No! I only know it from Steve Martin's "Saturday Night Live" sketch.

GEHRY The real reason I did the "Art Treasures from Japan" installation was that I didn't have any work in 1965. Of course, I was also interested in Japan. Greg Walsh, who worked with me at the time, was sort of an expert on Japanese art and culture. He had lived there for three or four years, and I think that's why George Kuwayama, who was curator of Asian art at the time, decided to bring us in to work on the installation.

FORSTER Over the years, your installations got to be more and more about architectural ideas, about making museum buildings. The German Expressionist Sculpture exhibition was in fact a kind of museum in bits and pieces.

GEHRY Well, yes.

FORSTER Pieces that could be fitted into existing buildings.

GEHRY But when the Museum of Contemporary Art (MoCA) was founded in Los Angeles (1980), it was the artists who rejected me. You know the story, don't you?

FORSTER No, I don't think I do.

GEHRY It was the most painful thing for me. I had worked with the Weismans to try and create a museum in Venice, but the idea was rejected by both the planning commission and the coastal commission. Marcia and Fred tried to get the Pan-Pacific Auditorium, and asked me to do a study. I did a lot of work analyzing how the building could be made to work as a museum. But I came to the conclusion that it would have to be torn down, because it was obvious that you would have to rebuild it anyway, and you would end up with nothing more than a facade. Marcia Tucker got a committee together, Gary Familian, Eli Broad, and Max Palevsky, with the idea of starting a contemporary art museum downtown. Mayor Bradley was involved. And then I heard, the day after a meeting at DeWain Valentine's studio with Mayor Bradley, that they had inaugurated MoCA, and I hadn't been invited. It was just for artists, Ed Moses, and Robert Graham, and Robert Irwin, and the rest of the them. I remember calling Marcia and saying, "You had a big meeting about a museum and you didn't invite me?"

And she said, "It was only for artists." And Marcia, to her dying day, never thought of me in any other way. I was the architect, I was different, and that was that. She loved me, but she wanted to keep me in my place. I then heard that Max Palevsky had given a million dollars to select the architect, and that Sam Francis was promoting Isozaki. Sam and I had worked together on the Jung Institute project years before. I also heard that Robert Irwin and Coy Howard were involved, and that they were planning to select Arata Isozaki. I got a phone call one night not too long afterward. I remember getting into New York, going into my hotel room, and the phone is ringing. It was Max Palevsky saying "Frank, I need a big favor from you." We're going to select an architect for MoCA and we need to interview five other architects with Isozaki. We're probably going to give it to Isozaki, but we need to interview a Los Angeles architect, and we would like you to be interviewed. You won't get the job, it's just to make it look good. And instead of saying something unprintable to Max, I agreed to be interviewed. Sam Francis was there, and Robert Irwin, Coy Howard, and Palevsky. I had the most fun I've ever had in an interview. I told them all the things that were going to happen. I predicted everything that did happen. Because it was obvious that the Japanese guy wouldn't understand the business relationship, and that the big guy developers were going to.....

FORSTER Disappear from the picture?

GEHRY Everything I told them eventually happened. I said "You need somebody a lot tougher with these guys or you're going to get beaten up in the construction process, and you won't even see it happening until it's too late."

FORSTER It's amazing that you put yourself through this.

GEHRY Well, it wasn't self-serving. I just thought that the right thing to do was to be bigger than this petty situation. Then I met Isozaki, got to know him, and liked him a lot. I still like him. But I found out that the artists had dumped me. Irwin, Berlant, Moses, Graham, Alexis Smith, the people I had considered to be friends for many years. I was very hurt. I found out later, because somebody weaseled. There is always a weasel. Someone called and said, "Frank, we've been to the meeting, and guess what they said about you? It was painful and it hurt, and I think it took me a couple of years to overcome my feelings about it.

Frank O. Gehry, Geffen Contemporary, Interior,
1995–1997, formerly: Temporary Museum of
Contemporary Art, Los Angeles, California

Frank O. Gehry, Geffen Contemporary, Exterior,
1995–1997, formerly: Temporary Museum of
Contemporary Art, Los Angeles, California

FORSTER Do you think it was just competition?

GEHRY I figured out a reason. The reason was that, as long as I was the
architect hanging out with the artists, I knew my place. They knew I was
talented, and they supported me. But as soon as they realized that I had
ambitions, that I wasn't just a wallflower and I was going for it in my own
way, it freaked them out a little.

FORSTER Of course, they had an easier time venting their anxieties about
competition with one person they had in common, rather than among each
other, right?

GEHRY Right. And they wanted to design it themselves. Robert Graham
really thought he could design a museum. He actually made a proposal. He

Frank O. Gehry, Geffen Contemporary, Exterior,
1995–1997, formerly: Temporary Museum of
Contemporary Art, Los Angeles, California

collaborated with Tony Berlant and Ed Moses. But then they called me when Isozaki was already well along with his work. It was Sam Francis who called to say they wanted to have dinner with me, he and Pontus Hulten and Richard Koshalek. I asked "What do you want to talk about?" We had dinner at a Japanese restaurant. They were all smiles, and said "We know we were terrible to you, and it wasn't fair, but we have a project for you that will make it all better. And we predict that this project will turn out to be more important than the one Isozaki is building." And they offered me the Temporary Contemporary (1982/83; renovations currently ongoing) in downtown Los Angeles. It was to be built from a couple of abandoned warehouses beyond the railroad station which had originally been a storage facility and a police vehicle repair depot.

Francis and Hulten and Richard Koshalek offered me this as a kind of consolation prize, and I said, "You guys keep adding insult to injury. What do you want from me?" But they insisted. This was going to be the best opportunity, it would save me, make me." So I said, "Well, let me think about it. I'll sleep on it." Next morning at eight o'clock my phone rang. It was Coy Howard saying "Did they offer you the Temporary Contemporary?" I said "Why? What are you talking about? Why do you want to know?" "It's my job," he said. "It was promised to me." And I said "Go tell them that." I hung up. And then I called them and said, "What kind of game is this any-way? Here's this kid who's been hanging around waiting for the museum job. Now he's paid his dues. You promised him the thing, and he's earned it." I hung up again. I was mad. Anyway, they waited a few days and they called back and they said "Look, we're not going to give it to him. Nobody else can handle it, it's your job, you've got to do it." They sent emissaries and tried all the tricks they could think of. And finally, I said "OK, but, what is there to do? Clean the floor?" On the inside, I just followed the logic of the building. The columns, the ramps and all that stuff were already there. But they were right, the Temporary Contemporary did it. I mean, precisely what I didn't do was more important than anything I did do. And shows looked good in there. I'm still involved with the thing. Now I'm proposing to take out all the ramps. But when Isozaki eventually ran into trouble, Pontus Hulten and Sam Francis called me to a meeting at Sam's studio, and they said, "You've got to help us. Isozaki is going to fail. He needs help." And I

Frank O. Gehry, Frederick R. Weisman Art and
Teaching Museum, Interior, 1990–1993,
Minneapolis, Minnesota

said, "Well, what do you want me to do. He's designing it." "This is so
important to art here and around the world. You're the only one who can
help him. He trusts you. You like him." They brought me to Iso. He was at
the Shangri-La Hotel in Santa Monica, it was midnight. I was sitting there in
the room with Iso and his wife, and I said to Francis and Hulten, "Would
you please leave and let me talk to him." And so I said to him "Do you really
want me to help?" And he said "Yes. I think it's going to fail." So I gave him
a pep talk. I said "Iso, you've got to fight, you've got to take a stand. You're
in the driver's seat. Don't let these guys push you around. It's too far into
the process; they can't go back. You've got all the aces. Fight!" So he
promised me he would fight. The next morning Sam Francis called me and
asked "What happened? Are you doing it? Are you going to help us?"
I said "Sam, give me a break. I'll help him, technically. We'll give it whatever
it takes, but it's his project." So I assigned one of my guys, who went
to meetings with Iso, figured out what was going wrong, and advised him.
Iso, being as Japanese as ever, resisted politely, but there are moments
when I still think about what happened to me with the artists. I never went
to see Sam when he was sick. Irwin and I have been estranged. I stopped
seeing Moses and Berlant. I just wrote them all off. We're friends again,
but it's never been the same. Then, a year or two ago, I ran into Irwin,
and he said "We made a big mistake, you should have done the whole
building."

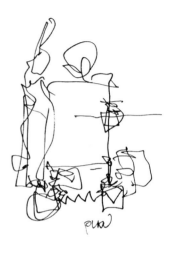

Frank O. Gehry, Frederick R. Weisman Art and Teaching Museum, 1990

Frank O. Gehry, Vitra Company, Headquarters,
1988–1994, Birsfelden, Switzerland

Frank O. Gehry, Vitra Design Museum,
1987–1989, Weil am Rhein, Germany

Frank O. Gehry, Vitra Design Museum, Interior,
1987–1989, Weil am Rhein, Germany

Frank O. Gehry, Cabrillo Marine Museum,
1977–1979, San Pedro, California

FORSTER The Frederick R. Weisman Art Museum (1990–1993) in
Minneapolis was really your first art museum.

GEHRY Yes, at Weil am Rhein (1987–1989) it was just a furniture museum
for Vitra. I had also done an aquarium many years ago in San Pedro, the
Cabrillo Marine Museum (1977–1979).

FORSTER Each of these projects was interesting for a different reason: the
Minneapolis project because of its urban campus location, the San Pedro
project for its laboratory atmosphere. But all of these aspects came together with the Bilbao Guggenheim (1991–1997).

GEHRY Bilbao has everything to do with the client, Tom Krens. He's a very
strong-willed guy with a vision. I think his vision grows out of North Adams,
the unbuilt project for the Massachusetts Museum of Contemporary Art

(1988) in North Adams. I know how he thinks. North Adams was a kind of premonition of Bilbao, because it had all these warehouse spaces and many differently shaped rooms and spaces. As he walked through it, Krens would talk about the spatial values. And he took those ideas to Bilbao. That's why we have a three-hundred-foot-long gallery there. There aren't rooms like that in New York.

FORSTER Yet Bilbao departs from the cliché of contemporary exhibition spaces. It's not a glorified loft. The Temporary Contemporary was basically a loft space. The Guggenheim in Bilbao is a completely different kind of museum. That's why it has become a hallmark of the city.

BECHTLER Why has the Guggenheim asked you to present a solution for hanging Rauschenberg's "Jacob's Ladder (1/4 Mile or 2 Furlong Piece)?"

GEHRY They are doing a major retrospective of Rauschenberg's work, and it will travel to Bilbao. Krens is worried about how to hang that quarter-mile-long painting. Rauschenberg is worried about it. No one knows how to do it. And they are fantasizing that somebody could figure out how to use the rotunda. So, they sent me a model of Frank Lloyd Wright's Guggenheim, and they're all sitting and waiting for me to solve their problem.

"I never thought that the spaces in museums were sacred, I only thought the art was sacred." Richard Serra

FORSTER We've talked about the importance of clients enabling you to engage them in a dance. Aren't you attributing a lot of power to them?

GEHRY More power, maybe, than they should have.

FORSTER That may well be. Why are you ready to involve your clients to such a degree?

GEHRY It depends on the client, you see. By the time I get a client who is ready to pay money to hire us and do something, they're pretty committed to whatever their fantasy might be. Then they discover two things. One is that we listen to their problems. I'm a good shrink. I listen. And the other thing is we listen to their budget. As soon as they feel comfortable, and if they're really interested…

FORSTER You come up with a result like the Winton guest house. There, you listened to the clients and gave them something with which they could begin to play.

GEHRY It was a really strong interaction, and when the clients are up to it, it can be very interesting. You've played the role of the client, so you know.

FORSTER I was wondering whether your involvement with artists was of a different nature. They want to make something, too. So how are they going to make it with you? When you work with an artist, you may find a more competitive or even antagonistic situation.

GEHRY The collaboration takes a different form. It's another kind of interaction. For the Lewis house, I made shapes that derive from my ING office tower in Prague (1995). Richard Serra saw them, because he came here often while I was working on it; he was intrigued and made two models of his own. I was also looking back at Oldenburg's Knees (though I wasn't conscious of it), and then here in my studio, he started making bags for golf clubs. He had begun to look at the same shapes Serra was interested in. Actually, it had all started with his own knees, I guess. So there is a process of fertilizing one another's imagination. Nobody got in anybody's way.

FORSTER This is clearly beyond the moment when Oldenburg would put a piece of his in front of one of your buildings, like in Weil am Rhein. At this level of interaction, you can no longer maintain demarcations. Your rapport with Serra and Oldenburg sets the objects themselves in motion.

GEHRY We got to feel how that kind of collaboration works with the Lewis house.

FORSTER Is that where you first reached this level?

GEHRY Yes, I've never experienced it before to the extent that we did there.

FORSTER So it's a double loss that the project was dropped by the client.

GEHRY And everybody's hurting because of it. The other day I heard Serra telling how it happened. I think he was telling Robert Hughes. We were both interviewed by Hughes, and we both told the same story forward and backward.

FORSTER So Hughes probably smelled a rat!

GEHRY In history, did that kind of thing happen?

FORSTER It happened only extremely rarely, and sometimes it happened without architect or artist realizing (or intending) what occurred. I'm thinking of Veronese painting his frescoes in the Villa Barbaro at Maser (1560s), or Tiepolo's ceiling in the giant vestibule of Schloss Würzburg (1760s), or El Lissitzky's installing a room for modern art in the Provinzialmuseum in

Hannover (1926/27). This is what is known in German as a Sternstunde, the fateful hour.

GEHRY But Saint-Gaudens, for example, working on the Chicago Exposition, must have had some kind of epiphany like that.

FORSTER It rarely reaches the point that you describe, where there is more than just a deep affinity between artist and architect, and something actually comes out of this mutual engagement.

"Actually Frank is courteous, considerate, and punctual, that coupled with his innate generosity and ferocious integrity makes it impossible to have a bad experience with him." Frank Stella

GEHRY Well, it happened. It happens anyway, but it doesn't always happen in the same time frame. If you see other people's work constantly, if you keep your eyes open, and you're influenced by other people's work, it will happen over time. Ours was a situation where we were playing, where there was a contextual game, where one person was creating a context, and the other person was responding to it. Then one person changed the context in response to the other. And so on, until pretty soon, there's this game going. I would love to figure out a way to keep it going, because, in the end, it makes everything so much richer.

Man Ray, Seguidilla, 1919, Hirshhorn Museum, Smithsonian Institution, Washington, D.C.

Stuart Davis, Percolator, 1927, The Metropolitan Museum, New York

FORSTER Oh yes. It's fundamentally different from taking a cue or a suggestion from a work of art at some distance in time, when the artist may not be around any more, or is not within reach, so that you react exclusively to an object. I would like to return to one aspect of your work that has intrigued me. I've often felt certain aspects of your work of the 1970s and early 1980s were a reaction to abandoned moments in American art, to things by Stuart Davis and Man Ray.

GEHRY Yes, I was looking at things like that.

FORSTER I'm sure you were, but what prompted you to look there when everybody was looking somewhere else? Of course, there were exhibitions and publications, but most architects seem not to have been interested in this at all. There must have been something about these peculiarly "American" influences.

GEHRY Yes, I was looking for an American thing, maybe because of the Hudnut experience at Harvard.

FORSTER Precisely at that moment when being an American was fraught with difficulties, you kept looking for a real "American" thing.

GEHRY I was looking for it, and I suppose these images did feel like that, whereas other things didn't. By then I had met Bob Indiana, and Jim Rosenquist.

FORSTER They, too, were picking up the line from Charles Demuth, from Stuart Davis, and Man Ray. This line began to assume more importance when you came into contact with Rosenquist and Indiana. But there is something else. We've talked about it in the past. It has to do with a special capacity to bring to attention things that have been completely overlooked, things in our immediate surroundings.

GEHRY Yes, I see that, but at the time, I wasn't conscious of it at all.

FORSTER That's exactly why you could exercise such power over these things. You brought latent, almost subterranean aspects of our culture to the surface. One may be struck by them when looking at photographs, especially photographs taken with no clear purpose, except perhaps to record the atmosphere of a place.

GEHRY I'll tell you two things about our culture that I was conscious of. One is that there was a lack of craftsmanship. I was trained by Victor Gruen to value Viennese perfection and detailing, but it was a lie. You couldn't do

Frank O. Gehry, Nationale-Nederlanden Building, 1992–1996, Prague

Frank O. Gehry, Nationale-Nederlanden Building, 1992–1996, Prague

it. You couldn't even get somebody to do it. You couldn't find craftsmen who were capable of doing it.

FORSTER True.

GEHRY So there was a disjunction between the object of desire and the reality of the times, the reality of production. That really angered me, because I'd been trained (my wrists were slapped if I deviated from those standards) to strive for something that I couldn't realize in my own work. I mean, some architects could realize it, like I. M. Pei, with the right kind of commercial client. But I'm talking about myself, the kind of clients I had when I started out. It just wasn't possible. On the other hand, Rauschenberg and Johns and all the other artists I was talking to and looking at were using junk in their paintings and sculptures. So I consciously said, "Well, if they can make stuff that sells in the galleries out of junk, then maybe I can too." At least it sparked me to think, "Look, maybe it doesn't have to be so perfect, maybe what we have is good enough; maybe it's even better." Because I tend to be a realist, I'll say, "If I can't do this, then I'll go another way." I don't sit around and fuss about it for very long. I just say "It's impossible. Okay, then. We've got to find another way." So we find another way. The same thing applies to the building of a city. Since I'd been to Harvard to study city planning, and since I didn't really want to build houses for wealthy people, I went through books of planners and urbanists who had graduated before me. I realized that many plans had already been conceptualized, but none of them were going to happen. And somehow I was sure of that. Even when I was working with Victor Gruen, I realized that these things weren't going to happen. They were just the stuff of pretty books. What was useful, though, was the dissemination of the ideas.

"The inside of Bilbao could have been even more radical, like the outside is. More sculpted rooms mixing with the conservative rooms." Walter De Maria

FORSTER Ideas and strategies.

GEHRY Yes, but the visual qualities were missing. I tried to figure out what that could mean to my work. What it turned out to mean is that visual chaos is a given, and I had to accept it, to live with it. Accepting it meant to try and make something happen in spite of it. If you had gone to Birsfelden, before my Vitra project was built there, you would have seen brick housing, buildings in wood, several villas at one end, a factory with this funny brick roof, a small office building three stories high, a little box, a couple of industrial buildings, the freeway, and the forest. I tried to insert a piece that would resolve all of it, that took its energy from this context. The odd thing is that, when people photograph my buildings, they usually crop the context.

FORSTER Actually, the Italian photographer Giovanni Chiaramonte changed that with his images for the little book I wrote about your work for Lotus International, America as Context. I encouraged him to capture the special relationship your buildings have with their often humdrum or chaotic settings, and in response, he developed a distinctive optic. Instead of isolating the buildings from anything and everything surrounding them, whether through the use of striking lighting effects, color, or cropping, he embedded them in their uncontrived situations. He even achieved a kind of fusion of the atmosphere of a place with the qualities of your buildings. With the Vitra International Headquarters (1988–1994) in Birsfelden, Switzerland, you resolved the conflict by giving center stage to chaos. You changed the nature of that particular chaos completely. What you got from those pretty books you were studying at Harvard is something that strikes most people as rigid, sterile, and exclusive of precisely those forces generated by life in the city.

Frank O. Gehry, Edgemar Development,
1984–1988, Santa Monica, California

GEHRY You can see this in what I did with the campus for the Loyola Law School (1978–1984) in Los Angeles. The existing buildings on Olympic Boulevard are all part of the composition.

"Frank commissioned me to design a stained glass ceiling for the non-denominational chapel which is part of the Loyola Law School project, but the client hated my design so they used something else." Jeremy Gilbert-Rolfe

FORSTER Just before coming here, Cristina Bechtler and I made a quick stop at the Edgemar Center in Santa Monica (1984–1988). It is a marvelous example, one that puts traditional notions of context to shame. You took the American storefront and gave it a tremendous new coherence and power.

GEHRY I think that's the essence of what I'm trying to do in every project. And you'll see it in Bilbao. The building really connects the city to the river, to the bridge.

FORSTER If all the things that impinge upon that site, the railroad, automobile traffic, wind, could give shape to one single thing, something like your museum would have to emerge.

GEHRY Right.

FORSTER Sometimes you see a piece of paper changing shape as it travels in the wind, bending and flying, sliding and billowing with the forces playing upon it, like a ballet. This is the way I would portray your architectural ideas when you put them to work in a given place. But precisely because of your approach to place, I'm surprised that theatrical and cine-

Frank O. Gehry, Set for Lucinda Child's Dance
Performance "Available Light", 1983, in the
Temporary Museum of Contemporary Art,
Los Angeles, California

Frank O. Gehry, Hollywood Bowl Renovations,
1970–1982, Hollywood, Los Angeles,
California

matic minds are not more numerous among your circle of friends and col-
laborators. Twenty years ago, people like Robert Wilson were already trying
to bring certain of these ideas to the stage.

GEHRY Well, Wilson and I have been friends that long.

FORSTER You haven't mentioned him.

GEHRY No, I know.

FORSTER Is that because it's not very important?

GEHRY I don't think so. It's just that I'm very wary of such references. I
remember once, when Isozaki gave his first lecture here in Los Angeles, he
showed the Campidoglio in Rome and compared it to one of his own buildings where he had tried to use certain ideas.

FORSTER Yes. That wouldn't be a favorable comparison.

GEHRY It doesn't work, so I rarely try it.

FORSTER You needn't, either. Your references are of a different order altogether.

GEHRY You can't be sure whether you would come out on an equal footing, you know?

FORSTER I think you can relax those fears. I was thinking of something
else, of how theater has transformed architecture. Today, urban chaos sur-
rounds us on all sides, there is no retreating back behind the window
frame. Something in the nature of your buildings conjures up the idea of
performance, of mutable and dynamic relationships, of dramatically changing manifestations.

GEHRY Seems so obvious to me that we don't need to talk about it.

FORSTER Still, I wonder why you never designed sets for a film or theater production, except the setting for the Available Light collaboration (1983) with Lucinda Childs and John Adams at the Temporary Contemporary in Los Angeles, and the cardboard sono-tube installations and new shell for the Hollywood Bowl (1970–1982).

GEHRY Well, nobody's asked. Actually, someone did, but it was the wrong person. Maybe I would be ready now. Ernest Fleischmann and Peter Hemmings asked me to do opera sets, but I turned them down. David Hockney can afford to do operas because he makes tons of maquettes and drawings, and they sell well in the galleries, so he doesn't care if he only gets twenty thousand dollars to do an opera. He takes a year out of his life to do it, but then he sells all the work and makes out fine because he also loves to do it. I would love to do it, too.

FORSTER Take a precedent like Fellini's "Casanova." They used sheets of black plastic to simulate the sea churning in a storm. The whole effect was achieved with the dregs of urban chaos, garbage bags standing in for the sea, and so on. Maybe it's too late now, but I could imagine that you would have a field day creating sets for a film.

GEHRY I would have done it, had someone come forward with a reasonable proposal.

FORSTER I even see connections to such things as your chairs. Stability is not the theme. But they are.....

BECHTLER They're alive.

FORSTER They're little vignettes of compression and elasticity. But let's talk for a moment about where your buildings are located. Basically, all over the world. That is certainly a recent phenomenon, that an architect's work can be almost anywhere in the world. Stirling built interesting work in Germany and those circumstances very much propelled his thinking. Norman Foster and Richard Rogers built in France and in Asia, Peter Eisenman—in internal exile—built in Ohio. You build on a global scale.

GEHRY But it's all happened in the last five or ten years.

FORSTER Yes, and it has happened in such a startling fashion, and in so many places.

GEHRY In Germany, it is really strange. You get the kind of clients who would build, but you also get the kind of clients who try to kill you. In general I think people are better educated about architecture in Europe. The tradition is more established. If you're rejected in Europe, you're rejected intelligently. Here, you're rejected because people are scared.

FORSTER That's an interesting distinction, because you tap into the contemporary urban experience and everything associated with it, change, chaos, transformation. You would expect it to play better at home.

GEHRY But most people hate it.

FORSTER Because it's perhaps the single most unifying experience common to all people in the world. There are monstrous avatars of the metropolis on every continent.

GEHRY I'll tell you what I think. I tell people, "This is what you do. This is what we do. I'm taking your language making it into something better. I'm taking your junk and making something with it." But they don't like it. It's just like the chain-link thing.

"The Bilbao Guggenheim Museum is the most awesomely man-built space I have ever experienced. It spiritually enlightens man and inspires art." Robert Rauschenberg

FORSTER Seemingly enough of them do want it.

GEHRY There are a few.

FORSTER Enough for you to go on doing this in many places. In some sense, Eisenman would say the same things. He went to Ohio, where there was not much to be found, streets, railroad tracks, highways, offramps, airport runways, etc. He built a convention center, picking up these pieces and bundling them up: "Here is your convention center." Much the same could be said of some of your own projects.

GEHRY Same thing. Right.

FORSTER Why, then, does it turn out to be very different? If you think you scare them, he's scared them clear away. So what's the difference?

"I think he has developed his own unique vocabulary which happens not so often in one's lifetime." Robert Wilson

GEHRY I think it's probably personality. I don't have the need like he does to torture them when they use the building. In the Wexner Center, for example, Eisenman made it so that people who worked there would have to look down a certain way to see the view. I mean, I wouldn't think to do that. I'm more user-friendly.

FORSTER You want me to believe that?

GEHRY Well, maybe it's not true. But it is true that I'm more giving and forgiving.

FORSTER So, would you measure your success by the degree of acceptance you have attained with the public?

GEHRY Well, I knew I had finally made it when I was in a cartoon in the New Yorker magazine. And one time, when I was in Europe, I was saying to a person who thought I'd achieved everything, "No, there's one thing I haven't achieved. I haven't had one of my buildings put into one of those little glass spheres with snowflakes inside, a snow-globe. You shake it up and then watch the snowflakes settle around whatever's been put inside." When I came back to Santa Monica, one was sitting on my desk.

FORSTER So which building was inside the sphere?

GEHRY The Weisman Museum. Talking about snow and ice, I designed an ice rink for the Disney Corporation, Disney Ice in Anaheim (1993–1995).

FORSTER A hockey rink?

GEHRY Yeah, and Mickey Mouse was there for the inauguration.

FORSTER And you were on the evening news?

GEHRY No, but tomorrow night we're playing ice hockey with Disney.

FORSTER With Mickey Mouse?

GEHRY With Mickey Mouse.

FORSTER Do they have a whole team, in full costume?

GEHRY Oh, I don't know. But I have a team, a hockey team.

FORSTER And this photograph?

"He is an architect thinking like a sculptor with his own signature."
Robert Wilson

GEHRY That's me playing hockey with my kids Alejandro and Sami. They're better than me. Alejo is at college, the Rhode Island School of Design, so he plays on the team there. Sami plays with me. We're playing Disney, because we did the rink. They challenged us.

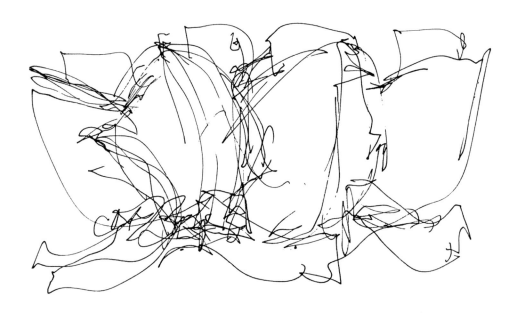

Frank O. Gehry, Study for the Disney Concert Hall in Los Angeles, 1991

Frank O. Gehry and Peter Eisenman at The Four
Seasons, New York, August 1991

FORSTER Who is on their team?

GEHRY I don't know, but I'm sure they have some ringers.

FORSTER I was just going to say.

GEHRY We've got ringers too!

FORSTER People from the office?

GEHRY No, we've got some former National Hockey League guys to play with us. There's the whole team over there.

FORSTER You're doing Peter Eisenman one better. He has phantom football teams; you have a real hockey team!

GEHRY Yeah, the real thing! Peter is very jealous.

FORSTER He is very jealous because he wished he had one.

GEHRY He doesn't care about my architecture, but this really gets him.

FORSTER That's not exactly true.

GEHRY No, no. He and I get along really well.

FORSTER I imagine Eisenman is one of the players out there who share the ice with you. So many architects seem to be shuffling around, but a few, a Siza in a silent corner and a Koolhaas in the noisiest stadium, pursue their own games. You play with different pucks, but you're playing the only game worth the risk.

Edited by Denise Bratton

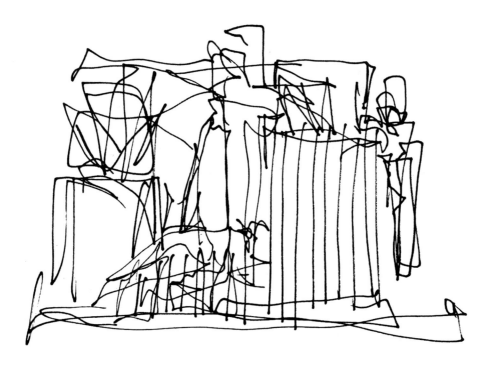

Frank O. Gehry, Study for the American Center in Paris, 1989

Philip Johnson, Glass House, 1947–1949, New Canaan, Connecticut

Giorgio Morandi, Still-Life, 1955, Morat-Institut für Kunst und Kunstwissenschaft, Freiburg im Breisgau, Germany

Frank O. Gehry, Summer Camp Good Times, Model, 1984/85, Santa Monica Mountains, Malibu, California

Dance Piece "Available Light" by Lucinda Childs, 1983, staged at the inauguration of Frank O. Gehry's Temporary
Museum of Contemporary Art, Los Angeles, California

Aldo Rossi, Il Teatrino Scientifico, Model, 1978

Edward Weston, Waterfront, 1946, Monterey, California

Frank O. Gehry, Wosk Residence, 1981–1984, Beverly Hills, Los Angeles, California

Frank O. Gehry, Guggenheim Museum Bilbao, 1991–1997, Bilbao, Spain

Frank O. Gehry, Guggenheim Museum Bilbao, 1991–1997, Bilbao, Spain

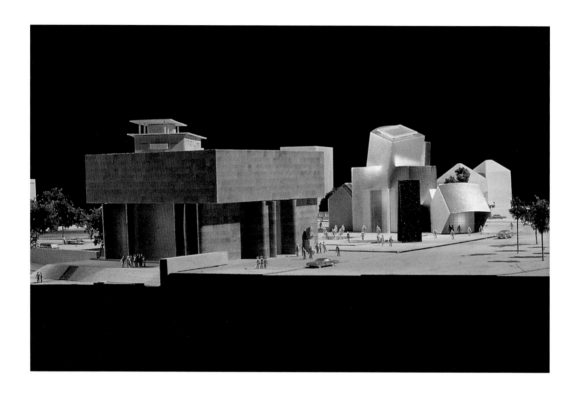

Frank O. Gehry, Kunsthalle Bielefeld, Addition (to the right), 1994, with Philip Johnsohn's Museum (to the left)

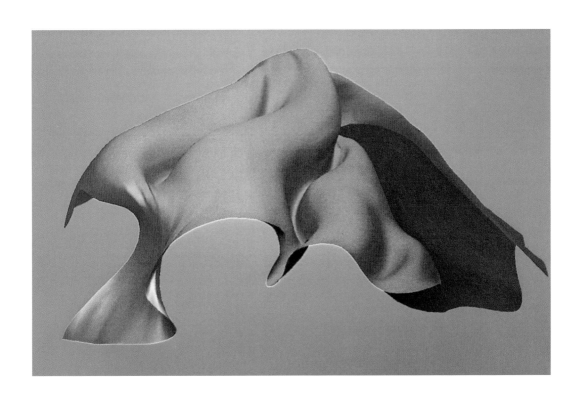

Frank O. Gehry, Lewis Residence, Computer-generated Study for the Atrium, 1995

John Chamberlain, Velvet White, 1962, Collection of Mr. and Mrs. Albert A. List

Frank O. Gehry, Gehry House, 1977–1979, Santa Monica, California

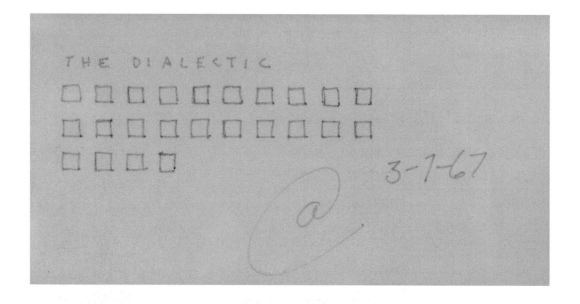

Carl Andre, The Dialectic, 1967, Collection of Frank O. Gehry

Carl Andre, Lever, 1966, The National Gallery of Canada, Ottawa, Ontario

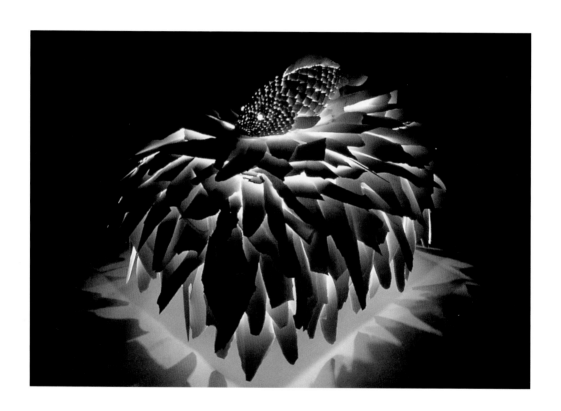

Frank O. Gehry, Fish Lamp, 1983

Frank O. Gehry, Seventeen Artists in the Sixties, 1981, Los Angeles County Museum of Art, California

Frank O. Gehry with Richard Serra, Millennium Bridge, Project, 1996, London

Frank O. Gehry with Richard Serra, Millennium Bridge, Project, 1996, London

Coosje van Bruggen, Frank O. Gehry and Claes Oldenburg, Il Corso del Coltello, 1985, Venice, Italy
Frank O. Gehry in his Costume as Architect "Frankie P. Toronto"

Frank O. Gehry, Prison: The Folly, Model, 1983

Frank O. Gehry, with Claes Oldenburg and Coosje van Bruggen, Model for the Chiat/Day/Mojo Building, 1991, Venice, California

Frank O. Gehry, with Claes Oldenburg and Coosje van Bruggen, Chiat/Day/Mojo Building, Binoculars, 1991, Venice, California

Frank O. Gehry, Frederick R. Weisman Art and Teaching Museum, 1990–1993, Minneapolis, Minnesota

Snow Globes with a Miniature Model of the Frederick R. Weisman Art and Teaching Museum

Frank O. Gehry, Nationale-Nederlanden Building, 1992–1996, Prague

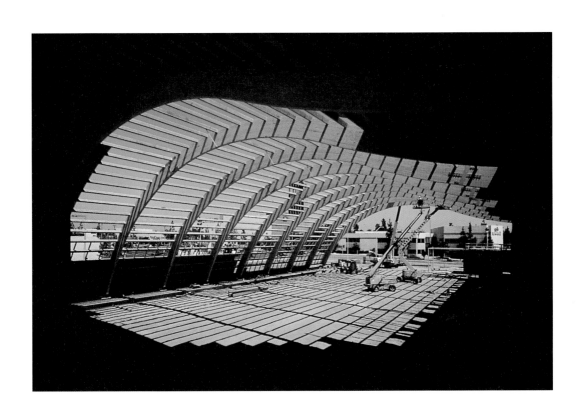

Frank O. Gehry, Disney Ice, Rink under construction, 1993–1995, Anaheim, California

Frank O. Gehry, Loyola Law School, 1978–1984, Los Angeles, California

Frank O. Gehry, Loyola Law School, 1978–1984, Los Angeles, California

Robert Rauschenberg, The 1/4 Mile or 2 Furlong Piece, 1981–1998, 178 Individual Elements on Mixed Media, Collection of the Artist, Installed in Frank O. Gehry's Guggenheim Museum Bilbao

Appendix

FRANK O. GEHRY

Frank O. Gehry and Associates, Inc., was established in 1962. Before founding the firm, Gehry worked for architects Victor Gruen and Pereira & Luckman in Los Angeles, and with André Rémondet in Paris.

The architecture studio has a staff of over ninety people, which includes a group of senior architects who are highly qualified in project management and in the technical development of building systems and construction documents, as well as extensive model-making facilities.

Raised in Toronto, Canada, Frank O. Gehry moved with his family to Los Angeles in 1947. He received his Bachelor of Architecture degree from the University of Southern California, and he studied City Planning at the Harvard University Graduate School of Design. In a career spanning four decades, Gehry produced public and private buildings in America, Europe and Asia. Gehry is particularly concerned that the people feel comfortable within the spaces he creates, and that this buildings respond to their sites and cultural context.

His work has earned Gehry several of the most significant awards in the architectural field and his buildings have received over a hundred national A. I. A. awards.

Recent and current projects include: the Guggenheim Museum Bilbao, Spain; Pariser Platz 3, a mixed-use building adjacent to the Brandenburg Gate in Berlin, Germany; the Neue Zollhof, an office complex in Dusseldorf, Germany; the Experience Music Project in Seattle, Washington; the Nationale-Nederlanden Building in Prague, Czech Republic; the Walt Disney Concert Hall in Los Angeles, California.

KURT W. FORSTER

Kurt W. Forster has taught the history of art and architecture at Yale, Stanford, M. I. T., and the Federal Institute of Technology in his native Zurich. He was the founding director of the Getty Research Institute for the History of Art and the Humanities in Los Angeles (1984–1992) and now heads the Canadian Centre for Architecture in Montreal. In addition to his studies on Renaissance and early modern architecture, he has written extensively on, and also collaborated with, architects like Peter Eisenman, Richard Meier, Daniel Libeskind, and Frank O. Gehry.

CRISTINA BECHTLER

Cristina Bechtler is a publisher and curator of exhibitions; she lives in Zurich. Besides the book series "Art and Architecture in Discussion," she also publishes various monographs and artists' books, such as Sol LeWitt and Matthew Barney.
1998 she founded INK TREE EDITION, which produces bibliophile books in collaboration with contemporary artists.

Bibliography
Kurt W. Forster about Frank O. Gehry

"Coals in the Snow—Floating Rocks. A Mountain Lodge at Telluride by Frank O. Gehry", *Casabella,* 662/663, 1998.

Frank O. Gehry and Kurt W. Forster—A Dialogue, ed. by Cristina Bechtler, Ostfildern-Ruit 1998.

"Coreografia architettonica", *Frank O. Gehry. Tutte le opere,* Milan 1998, pp. 9–37; English: New York 1998; German: Stuttgart 1998.

"Bilbao-Song. Frank Gehrys Guggenheim Museum in Kantabrien", *Parkett,* 50/51, 1997, pp. 261–270.

"Lungo i sentieri dell'immaginazione: architetture di Frank Gehry a Los Angeles. Along the Boardwalk of Imagination: Frank Gehry's Buildings in Los Angeles", *Frank O. Gehry: America come contesto. America as Context (Quaderni di Lotus),* ed. by Mirko Zardini, 20, 1994.

"Siège social Vitra: une architecture pour le plaisir et le travail", *Frank O. Gehry: Projets en Europe. Album de l'exposition,* Paris 1991.

"Choreographie des Zufalls. Choréographie du hasard", *Archithese,* 1, 1991, pp. 16–29.

"Federnder Widerstand. Neue Stühle von Frank Owen Gehry", *Archithese,* 1, 1991, pp. 61–64.

"Pictures from an Architectural Pantomime. Taferelen uit een Architecturale Pantomime", *Forum International,* 6, 1991, pp. 40–49.

"Pictures from an Architectural Pantomime. Espacios coreográficos: Imágenes de una pantomima arquitectónica", *Frank Gehry 1985–1990. A & V,* 25, 1990, pp. 13–16.

"The Snake and the Fish on the Hill. Walt Disney Concert Hall, Los Angeles, 1988", *a+u/ Architecture and Urbanism,* 239, 1990, pp. 34–52.

"La serpiente y el pez en la colina: El auditorio de Gehry", *Arquitectura Viva,* 10, 1990, pp. 27–31.

"The Snake and the Fish on the Hill. Il pesce e il serpente al vertice, a proposito del progetto Gehry", *Zodiac,* 2, 1989, pp. 180–195.

"Visionen urbaner Transparenz. Zu Frank Gehrys Konzerthallen-Projekt für Los Angeles. Visions of Urban Transparency. On Frank Gehry's Concert Hall Project for Los Angeles", *Daidalos,* September 1989, pp. 26–35.

"Goldberg Variations. A Commentary to Frank Gehry's Drawings", *Frank O. Gehry. Design Museum Vitra, Weil am Rhein,* Berlin 1989, pp. 8–9.

"Volumi in libertà: Frank Gehrys architektonische Improvisationen", *Archithese,* 3, 1988, pp. 53–58.

"Improvisations on Locations", *The Architectural Review,* 182, 1987, pp. 65–66.

"California Architecture: Now You See it, Now You Don't", *Edge Condition. UCLA Architecture Journal,* Special issue, 1986, pp. 5–22.

Photo Credits

American Masterworks – The Twentieth Century
   House, ed. by Kenneth Frampton and David
   Larkin, New York 1995, p. 112: p. 97
Carl Andre – Sculpture 1959–1977, New York 1978,
   p. 51: p. 111
Pamela Blackwell © J. Paul Getty Trust: p. 6
H. Blessing: p. 35 bottom left
Richard Bryant: p. 82 top left
Giovanni Chiaramonte: p. 119
Esto: pp. 82 top right, 82 bottom right
FMGB Guggenheim Bilbao Museoa, Erika Barahona
   Ede: p. 126
FOG/A: pp. 16, 27 top right, 30, 31 left, 34, 35 top,
   36 bottom right, 44, 49 top, 64 right, 67, 74 top
   right, 74 bottom left, 75, 78, 82 bottom left,
   87, 89 f., 99 f., 103, 106, 110, 112 f., 116–118,
   121 f., 125
Hugh Hales-Tooke: p. 95
David Heald: pp. 36 top, 36 bottom left, 104 f.
Grant Mudford: pp. 23, 27 top left, 27 bottom right,
   35 bottom right, 68, 210
The New Yorker: p. 4
Marvin Rand: pp. 74 top left, 74 middle, 74 bottom
   right
Recent American Sculpture, New York 1964, p. 18:
   p. 108
Arturo Schwarz, The Complete Works of Marcel
   Duchamp, London 1969, p. 254: p. 33
J. Scott Smith: p. 96
Staatliche Museen zu Berlin, Kupferstichkabinett
   und Sammlung der Zeichnungen: p. 24 top left

Tim Street Porter: pp. 27 bottom left, 124
Jim Strong, New York: p. 49 bottom right
Elisabetta Terragni, Como: p. 21
Lamberto Vitali, Morandi – Catalogo Generale, vol.
   2, Mailand 1977, p. 944: p. 98
Don F. Wong: pp. 81 f., 120

All other illustrations derive from the archive of
Kurt W. Forster.

Impressum

Edited by Cristina Bechtler
Translations: Melissa Thorson Hause
Graphic Design: Saskia H. Rothfischer
Production: Christine Müller
Reproduction: Repromayer, Reutlingen

Printed by Dr. Cantz'sche Druckerei, Ostfildern-Ruit

Published by
Cantz Verlag
Senefelderstraße 12
D-73760 Ostfildern-Ruit
Tel. 0049/711/4405–0
Fax 0049/711/4405–220
Internet: www.hatje.de

Distribution in the US
D.A.P., Distributed Art Publishers, Inc.
155 Avenue of the Americas, Second Floor
USA-New York, N.Y. 10013–1507
Tel. 001/212/6271999
Fax 001/212/6279484

ISBN 3-89322-963-9 (English edition)
ISBN 3-89322-331-2 (German edition)

Printed in Germany

Die Deutsche Bibliothek - CIP-Einheitsaufnahme

Frank O. Gehry / Kurt W. Forster. Ed. by Cristina Bechtler in
collab. with Kunsthaus Bregenz. [Transl.: Melissa Thorson Hause].
- Ostfildern-Ruit : Cantz, 1999
   (Art and architecture in discussion)
   ISBN 3-89322-963-9